Karma Kids

Answering Everyday
Parenting Questions
with Buddhist Wisdom

Greg Holden

Ulysses Press

Published by: Ulysses Press
P.O. Box 3440
Berkeley, CA 94703
www.ulyssespress.com

Library of Congress Control Number: 2004101019
ISBN 1-56975-419-5

Printed in Canada by Transcontinental Printing

10 9 8 7 6 5 4 3 2 1

Interior design: Jilly Sitford, 'Ome design
Cover design: Leslie Henriques
Cover photograph: Ryan McVay/Gettyimages.com

Distributed in the United States by Publishers Group West and in Canada by
Raincoast Books

The author has made every effort to trace copyright owners. Where he has
failed, he offers his apologies and undertakes to make proper acknowledgment
where possible in reprints.

The recipe on page 35 is reprinted with permission from *The Kopan Cookbook:
Vegetarian Recipes from a Tibetan Monastery* by Betty Jung (San Francisco:
Chronicle Books, 1992)

This book has been written and published strictly for informational purposes,
and in no way should it be used as a substitute for consultation with your
medical doctor or a health care professional. All facts in this book came from
medical files, clinical journals, scientific publications, personal interviews,
published trade books, self-published materials by experts, magazine articles,
and the personal-practice experiences of the authorities quoted or sources
cited. You should not consider educational material herein to be the practice
of medicine or to replace consultation with a physician or other medical
practitioner. The author and publisher are providing you with information in
this work so that you can have the knowledge and can choose, at your own
risk, to act on that knowledge.

CONTENTS

Introduction: Parenting the Buddhist way

My nine-year-old daughter and I have an ongoing contest. My announcement that I am going to take a shower is her signal to cause some mischief. The shower, for me, is not just a time for cleansing. I take the opportunity of solitude and focus to do a little meditation. In the middle of my peaceful, enlightened state, Lucy flushes the toilet. My blissful shower suddenly turns boiling hot, then ice-cold. The first few times this occurred, my feelings of serenity and goodwill toward all humanity flew right out the bathroom window. Eventually, I came to realize that this was a test of my parenting abilities—in this case, a test of my patience. With practice, I became able to laugh it off and can now even play along, howling in mock protest as the temperature changes, much to my daughter's delight.

Have you ever noticed how, in the very moment when you are trying to relate closely to the kids and appreciate an instant of family togetherness, someone cuts you off in traffic, a telemarketer calls, or a glass of milk tumbles to the floor? I have come to believe that these moments all have something to teach us. Life constantly presents us with hardships and challenges; it is our job to turn them into opportunities that will help us to be better parents. Kids will pierce your ego and wreak havoc on your preconceptions and expectations if you only let them. They'll help you grow and progress spiritually as they do a dance that is alternately happy, complaining, demanding, and ecstatic (and that's just in a single hour). In return, you can help your children grow by recognizing and accepting them for who they are, by making them feel safe and nurtured, by helping them to appreciate what they have, and by teaching them consideration for all living things.

"A child is a bell of mindfulness, reminding us how wonderful life is."

Thich Nhat Hanh

What tools can help you do this? The most valuable parenting tools I know are generosity, patience, morality, enthusiasm, focused attention, and wisdom. As it happens, these tools are the Six Perfections of Buddhism—qualities all Buddhists strive to achieve. You don't have to be a monk to practice these qualities; they are everyday virtues that can help anyone live better. The Buddhist ideas you will find in this book can help you listen to your children, face everyday frustrations with greater equanimity, and help your child deal with the triumphs and tragedies of childhood and adolescence.

As the parent of two young daughters, I find few things more discouraging than reading a book that portrays spiritual parenting as all sweetness and light. There are plenty of books that attempt to apply New Age or Eastern religious principles to daily practice. But the authors often grow organic vegetables and visit the local monastery on a daily basis. Their children glowingly describe idyllic childhoods marked by their parents' constant wisdom and infinite patience. Let me tell you right up front that I'm not one of those Buddhist parents who follows the ideal of never getting angry. And, far from a shrine to perfect order and harmony, my house is a jumble of hamster cages, dollhouses, marbles, and musical instruments.

So what qualifies me to write about parenting the Buddhist way? Most importantly, just like you I am trying to be a better person and a better parent. I have been practicing and studying the dharma (the historical teachings of the Buddha and their real-life applications) for 15 years and am still struggling to integrate it into my daily life. I have studied with good teachers, and there are plenty of Buddhist parents among my friends whose wisdom and experience I am also happy to pass on to you. I have been blessed with two daughters who teach me and challenge me on a daily basis to practice patience, generosity, and other Buddhist perfections. Finally, I am a professional writer. The same skills that help me to make my living writing books about computers—the ability to convey ideas that are often complex and esoteric in simple, down-to-earth language—will help me translate some of the complexities of Buddhist teachings as well.

One of the first things that attracted me to Buddhism was the ease with which spiritual principles can be applied to one's daily activities through meditation and regular practice. Buddhism is an eminently practical religion and, accordingly, this is a practical book. Subtopics within each section present a variety of complementary activities that the whole family can do together.

Discussion starters

Discussion Starters, which you'll find throughout this book, are questions you can ask your kids to prompt a discussion about spiritual values. Sometimes kids are reluctant to voice their thoughts and feelings on their own. But they'll feel more at ease and be more willing to talk if you ask a question to stimulate their thoughts.

Stories to read aloud

Stories to Read Aloud are excerpts from or summaries of stories taken from Buddhist literature. These stories may be from Buddha's life or about Buddhism in general, and are perfect for reading during long car rides or at bedtime.

Things to do

Things to Do are suggestions for activities or projects that you and your kids can do together. Most have an end result that can be admired and enjoyed, but the real benefit is in bringing your family closer and staying connected to one another.

Exercises

The exercises throughout the book include activities or projects you might prepare alone or that you and your children can follow together. They are designed to provide concrete methods for putting into practice a principle being introduced in the section.

Although this book describes Buddhist ideas and practices, you don't have to be a Buddhist to benefit from it. This book can be a practical guide for Quaker, Jewish, and Christian families as well. In fact, all parents who admire Buddhism and who would like to apply its principles and lessons to their lives will benefit. Feel free to skip around and glean ideas that will work with your individual children or your specific circumstances. My techniques are general enough that anyone can use them in their own home. Filling water bowls is an exercise most young children will enjoy, as is going on a scavenger hunt or constructing a totem pole. Children can turn almost anything into a meditation cushion or practice ground. You don't have to wait for a special time or place to apply what you have learned about Buddhism. It is ideal for helping with any issues you encounter in daily life.

My goal is to stimulate your creativity so that you can adapt time-tested principles to your individual needs and take advantage of teachable moments that arise from day to day. The practice of Buddhism, after all, is not confined to one place or one ritual.

This book gives you tools that you can use in your daily life as you're taking your children to and from lessons, consoling them when they feel they have been wronged, or encouraging them to share. It will help you find ways to put the real-life religion of Buddhism into practice, guiding your children mindfully toward a balanced, happy childhood.

PART ONE

At home with the Buddha

Children these days are often overstimulated, overwhelmed, and overstressed. They are pressured to learn everything at an earlier age than ever before, and then grow up in a hurry. Children need a refuge: a place of peace, a place where they can feel safe and nurtured. At the same time, one's home should be a place where children can work out conflicts, learn good habits, and pursue "practical spirituality" by cleaning, helping, and sharing. The lives of busy Western parents make it difficult to achieve perfect order and harmony at home all the time. This section provides parents with tips and strategies for dealing with messiness, distractions, bickering, and fatigue in a mindful, patient way, regardless of their spiritual background.

Dealing with conflict

As a single parent raising two young girls, it often seems like I am on a long retreat—a period of time set aside for intense practice, discipline, and spiritual development. But there is a difference. This particular type of retreat has nothing to do with sitting cross-legged on my cushion meditating about anger, conflict, suffering, or clinging, and quietly generating compassion for all beings. Instead, I have a constant stream of irritation, impatience, jealousy, and attachment thrown in my face by my children. "Here, Daddy," they seem to say. "Time to practice patience! We chose the time when you would be most tired and stressed out just to give you an extra challenge. Try and be compassionate now!" It's like living in a spiritual boot camp—a charged atmosphere where clinging, impatience, or bickering can arise at any time. Kids know how to push your buttons. They will teach you to manage your anger and strengthen your patience whether you plan to or not. Realize that conflict around the house is okay. You can't walk around the house being little Buddhas. No one is perfect. Through conflict and challenge, you will grow.

When a dispute arises, pause before diving into your children's current drama. Sit quietly, if only for a moment or two, and set your mind on developing patience. Don't react right away. Try one of the exercises that follow. They are based on Buddhist principles and take different approaches to the anger and conflict that arise in virtually everyone's home from time to time.

EXERCISE

The circle game

When children or other members of the household are angry and fighting, one result is that nobody in the house can listen. The tension makes communication impossible. In his children's book entitled *Under the Rose Apple Tree*, the well-known Zen Buddhist teacher and former Vietnamese monk Thich Nhat Hanh suggests stopping and saying to oneself: "Breathing in, I am irritated. Breathing out, irritation is still there." Needless to say, it can be difficult to do this, because it runs counter to all of our usual patterns of behavior. We would rather yell, "Leave me alone!" or continue to fight or retreat to a corner. But simply breathing for a few moments produces change, and we become better able to listen to one another.

A friend of ours sets up the following exercise when children are experiencing a conflict. At first, it might seem strange, but I can tell you from experience that it works. When your children are arguing, either with siblings or friends, gather them all together and sit in a circle. Designate a special stick or token as the "talking stick." Pass the talking stick around from person to person. Whoever is holding the stick should say something about what happened or what they are feeling. The others just listen quietly until their turn comes. Let everyone have a turn to be heard.

The "talking stick" exercise doesn't have to be limited to conflict resolution. Once a child who was visiting our house suddenly bolted out the door and down the street. When we were unable to locate her right away, great consternation developed, especially among the parents in the group. After she returned— she had only taken a walk around the block to calm down—we all sat in a circle and passed the talking stick around. We agreed that, in the future, if a child felt the need for some space, she should tell an adult before heading outside. The tension faded away and everything was fine once again.

DISCUSSION STARTER

Did the Buddha ever get angry?

The quick answer is, Probably not. In fact, the Buddha said, "There is no non-virtue heavy like that of anger; there is no contemplation difficult like that of meditating patience" (Rimpoche, 353).

Devadatta, Buddha's jealous cousin, was continually trying to murder the Buddha by poisoning him or throwing rocks at him. Nothing seemed to harm the Buddha, however. Devadatta said to himself, "If the Buddha can eat all that poison, I can eat double that amount." He consumed a huge amount of poison and came very close to death. Buddha said, "If it is true that I have not had a single ounce of anger against him or a single bit of jealousy against him, I feel there is no difference between Devadatta and my son Rahula. If this is true, may he get better." Immediately, Devadatta recovered.

Is it possible to live a human life among other beings, to witness all the hatred and injustice in the world, and yet never become angry? Those of us who have spent time around great Tibetan lamas or teachers such as Thich Nhat Hanh understand that it is possible, since we have never seen these people become angry. The thing that children will hopefully take away from the preceding story is that they, too, can aspire to be like Buddha—to awaken within themselves their own capacities for avoiding anger and developing patience and love. By meditating and studying such universal principles, you can gradually change your own behavior. You will become angry less often and learn different ways to react to situations that used to make you feel irritated or outraged.

Practicing play-date generosity

Children often surprise us with their spontaneous generosity. They can also surprise us with their unconcealed selfishness. Inviting children to your house for after-school or weekend play dates, birthday parties, and the like is the perfect opportunity for your kids to practice play-date generosity.

At our house, disagreements nearly always arise over which game is to be played first, which role will be assumed by which child, which activity is acceptable to all participants, and so on. I encourage my daughters to be generous hosts. Since their friends are their guests, they should let their friends do what they want to do—at least, to begin with. Later on, they can switch to another game.

It's gratifying to see the children follow through with this idea. Sometimes I take the time to mention that generosity is the most important of the Six Perfections to which all Buddhists aspire. (The others are morality, patience, enthusiasm, focused attention, and wisdom.) Most of the time, I let my example do the talking. I give guests the first handful of popcorn or the first cookie and ask attentively if they would like some juice, hoping my children will follow accordingly. Kids can be encouraged to invent their own role-playing activities so as to extend generosity to people other than their immediate circle of friends. They can be generous with their own siblings by caring for them: giving them a hug, giving them a blanket when they are cold, or trying to cheer them up when they are out of sorts.

EXERCISE

Birthday gifts—with a twist

My daughters' elementary school has an interesting tradition that helps teach generosity. When someone has a birthday, he or she is invited to bring in treats for the whole class to share. The student (and his or her mother or father, or the teacher) hands out the gifts to everyone present. The class thanks the student by singing the traditional birthday song. Involving your son or daughter in the choosing, making, or distribution of these gifts extends attention outward, toward others, preventing the self-absorption that can sometimes make birthdays emotionally charged and often stressful.

EXERCISE

Becoming the calm rock of patience

When children are fighting with one another or with their playmates, it can be easy to get dragged into their conflicts. At least, it is for me. I try to mediate and negotiate and instead end up with a headache. More often than not, the kids work out their own disputes after I have given up in despair.

When conflicts occur, take a step back and watch how you react. My first impulse is to get involved—to exert control and authority, to nip fights in the bud. This doesn't teach the children to work out their own differences, however. Instead, it teaches them to be dependent on me for solutions to their problems.

My other reaction when a fight occurs is to raise my voice and issue the command: "Stop fighting!" Rather than being truly present for the children and giving them what they need, I sometimes sit back and yell. If the youngsters are hitting or calling each other names, they do require my involvement. If they are disagreeing over a game or a rule, they are better served by being allowed to work out their own problems.

Laziness, by the way, is one of the pitfalls of modern-day family life that the Buddhist author Jack Kornfield in a series of talks called "The Eightfold Path for the Householder" warns against. (See the Bibliography for more information on Kornfield's work.) The bored irritation that causes someone to yell without getting up or getting involved is a type of laziness. Instead of falling prey to this habit, focus on being fully present for your children. Kornfield suggests that you do this by first recognizing your own patterns of *not* being present for those around you. Once you have acknowledged that such patterns exist, you can begin to overcome them. Pay particular attention to these feelings:

- The desire for something new or different (Kornfield calls this the "If-Only Mind")
- Anger, which includes the desire to project our irritation, boredom, pain, or dissatisfaction on those around us
- Sleepiness, which includes being physically tired, but may also arise from being unhappy with what you are doing or with the situation around you
- Restlessness, which may arise from the speed and stimulation of modern culture, and which can keep us continually busy if we do not know how to be still
- Doubt, which arises when we begin to wonder about different choices without being connected to the love and true feelings that are in one's heart

Rather than getting dragged into fights, stop and listen. What's going on with the children? What are their genuine needs? It may be that some bickering gives them the chance to negotiate, to determine what they want, and to work things out on their own. Let them be cranky and blow off steam for a while. Take a deep breath, generate compassion for them, and do nothing. Don't get dragged into fights and jump up out of irritation that your own activities are being interrupted. It's perfectly natural to be irritated, but you can sit with that feeling for a few moments and acknowledge that, yes, you are irritated, without translating it into a negative reaction. As so often happens, your children can teach you if you only let them. In this case, they help you to practice patience.

When things get out of hand and it becomes obvious that your kids' powers of negotiation are inadequate for solving the problem at hand, you may get involved. But maintain the patience you have already developed. Calmly determine what is going on. You may have to ask one child to play in a different room for a while. If a child is hitting or calling names, you may have to escort that child home, explaining that these actions break the rules of behavior in the house. If the child is already home, give him or her a "time out" by sitting quietly and reflecting on what just happened and why it was wrong. Be sure to do so calmly and with compassion.

Precepts for the home

Buddhists observe a number of precepts. The most essential of these, as prescribed by the Buddha, are:

1. Do not destroy life
2. Do not steal
3. Do not commit sexual misconduct
4. Do not lie
5. Do not take intoxicating drinks

It's a good idea to post rules of behavior in your own house. How else can children know if they're violating a rule if they aren't aware of the rule in the first place? The following rules of cleanliness are posted at our house:

1. Any clay left on the floor will be thrown out immediately

2. Before you move on to the next thing, clean up what you have been doing
3. All dirty dishes must be put in the sink or dishwasher

I realize that some parents let children keep their own rooms as messy as they want. I have been one of those parents myself. After spending time looking for one toy or possession after another and watching the back seat of the car and other areas of the house become messy because the children have developed the habit of messiness, I have tried to take a more directive approach.

I have combined these rules to come up with a new and more age-appropriate set of precepts for household behavior:

1. Do not kill any living creature
2. Do not steal
3. Do not lie
4. Clean up before you move on
5. Do not hit
6. No name-calling
7. Be generous

The first precept involves respect for life, an especially powerful concept that can have a strong impact on children. Simply making a commitment to not killing spiders and other pests you find in the home, whenever possible, will give them a living example that vividly illustrates the importance of caring for other living beings. This idea is explained in more detail in Part Three ("Showing respect for life," pages 132–134).

When love and light are extinguished by aches and pains

The stereotypical image of Buddhists and other New Age practitioners is one of perpetually smiling, mellow, unfailingly generous individuals who seem to be dancing on air and continually speaking about love and light. Anyone who is trying to raise young children knows just how far removed he or she can be from this image. Parents are often physically and mentally worn-out. When your defenses are down, it's easy to snap at your children.

Give yourself the chance to be who you are. Being a mindful Buddhist (or Christian, or Muslim, or Hindu, or Jewish) parent does not mean you walk around happy all the time. It means being mindful of your own physical and mental well-being. "I'm especially stressed out today. I don't feel well. I'll try not to take it out on the kids." Simply acknowledge that you're not operating at 100 percent and take that into account when you deal with your kids' demands for food, money, or attention.

Your job as a parent is to do the best you can for your kids and to reduce your anger, not to be perfect all the time. It is not your place to make your children perfect, either, but to recognize them for who they are and accept them with their own imperfections. If you snap at the children, don't beat yourself up about it. Acknowledge to yourself that you were wrong. Tell them how you were feeling when you said what you did, and ask that they be mindful of this. Apologize if it is necessary—but only if it is truly necessary. Apologies should be handed out sparingly to children because of the danger that they will think you are inadequate or that they are in charge. There's a big difference between saying, "I'm sorry I yelled at you," and "I was feeling tired and impatient before, and that was why I yelled." The first statement conveys to your son or daughter only that you were *wrong*, which they take to mean that they are *right*. The second statement provides a context for your behavior and conveys the reasons you reacted in a certain way. The latter statement does not imply that the child was right, only that the *conditions* weren't right.

Remember that even if you forget to participate in a spiritual exercise with your children, if you miss a teachable moment and don't convey something important, or if you react with anger or impatience, you must still be compassionate with yourself. How can you forgive your children and extend loving kindness toward them if you are unable to give it to yourself? Remember, it's called spiritual *practice* because you need to practice it—you may not behave perfectly every time, but you are continuously improving.

Working through sadness and negative feelings

Young children are remarkably resilient. One minute they are crying about a friend who offended them or a pet cat that ran away, and the next they are involved in a new activity and smiling happily. *You* are likely to feel bad for your child long after he or she has already begun to move on. Helping children work through sadness often means providing a compassionate shoulder to cry on when needed and the space they need to move forward afterward. Some situations—particularly those involving divorce and separation—produce sadness and questions that aren't easily resolved. In case you encounter such questions or others related to impermanence and loss, the following exercises should help.

DISCUSSION STARTER

Why am I sad one moment and happy the next?

Children have intimate experience with impermanence, although they do not label it as such. Their
own moods come and go with the wind. One moment
they are filled with delight because a playmate has
arrived; the next they are pouting because of a few
choice words uttered by that same playmate. Helping
children recognize that change is a part of everyday
experience and that nothing is permanent can soften
the peaks and valleys of their own emotions.

DISCUSSION STARTER

My iguana died last year, so why am I still sad?

My own daughter still gets sad when she sees photos
of a cat that disappeared several years ago. I tell her
it's okay to feel sad, but that she should think a good
thought or say a prayer for the cat. I don't try and
negate her feelings, but I do try to turn them into
some sort of positive action so she feels some measure of empowerment.

DISCUSSION STARTER

My parents drive me nuts when we're together but I miss them when they go away. How I can feel close to them even when we're apart?

Tell your kids to take some tangible reminder of the absent parent and carry it around with them. They can take a photo and put it in their wallet or purse, or wear it in a locket around their neck. Carrying an object around helps give those feelings of loss a place to go.

Q. Why do I keep worrying that I'll never see my mom or dad again?

Q. I get so excited and then so sad; what's wrong with me?

Q. I can't stop thinking about someone. What can I do?

Q. Didn't the Buddha ever get angry?

EXERCISE

Letting go

Feelings of loss or disappointment can be even harder to let go when you try to ignore them. Acknowledging negative feelings will help your child move past them.

One memorable New Year's Eve, my *sangha* walked through the moonlit snow to a big bonfire. (The term sangha traditionally refers to a community of monks. In modern times, it has come to mean the group of people with whom you meditate and learn—a Buddhist spiritual community.) In our hands we held slips of paper on which we had described regrets, feelings of grief, and anything else we wanted to let go of in the coming year. When we reached the fire we threw the papers in, one by one. It was a powerful ritual that strongly affected all of those present—and it made me feel much better.

You don't need a bonfire when you or your children are trying to work though feelings surrounding the death of a pet, the loss of a favorite possession, a fight with a friend, or a similar situation. Use a barbecue pit or a backyard shrine if you have one. If not, place a metal cooking pot in your yard. Have your children write down on pieces of paper the feelings or objects they want to let go. Have them fold the paper and stand before the fire. Then throw the paper in the fire (or light it in the pot) and let it burn. As it burns, invite your children to picture the bad feelings leaving their minds and mingling with the smoke that rises into the air.

Putting the "family" back in family dinner

Cooking and eating together are activities that help define a family. Dinner is often the only time in the day when the whole household can sit together and talk. Your choices about what you eat and where you get it help convey your values to your child. If you have space for a vegetable garden, you might grow some of your own food with your children's help. Vegetable gardening gives your children the chance to appreciate bounty created by nature and their own hard work. When you shop at the store, you might choose as many natural, organic foods as possible. Eating local, seasonal fruits and vegetables creates a feeling of connection to the earth and its seasons. Many Buddhists are vegetarian, because respect for life is one of the central principles of Buddhism. Others choose a middle path, eating only animals that have been raised sustainably and killed humanely.

Preparation of the meal and the experience of sharing it can be a routine, a social gathering, or a spiritual experience. Most often, it's one of the first two. Once in a while, it might be the last. Traditional Buddhist blessings at mealtime involve visualizing turning the food into spiritual energy for helping others. At a meal when your children seem receptive, you might encourage them to think about the profound life-giving properties of food: "Let's imagine our bodies turning the food into energy. We can use the energy to help each other and the rest of the world."

Wash your hands

Most parents, when we have finished cooking and are spooning the evening meal onto plates or into bowls, have casually shouted up the stairs: "Wash your hands for dinner!" Most of the time, our command leads to a race to see which child can first get through a quick splash of water and a fast grasp of towel without ever touching soap.

Consider a more peaceful approach to washing hands. In many traditions, hand-washing represents cleansing the mind and body. You can adopt this ritual as a way of shedding the stresses of work and school before relaxing for the family meal. Introduce it to your children without anticipating resistance or making light of it. Your children will participate naturally and follow your example.

1. Prepare a pitcher, a bowl, and a towel. Designate a special pitcher and bowl for this purpose. (You might have fun shopping for these items with your kids.) Fill the pitcher with clean water.

2. Arrange the materials outside the dining area, so that the washing is done before entering the room.

3. Walk to the room where your children are playing. Calmly announce that dinner is ready and that the children need to wash their hands before eating.

4. When the kids arrive, direct them to the bowl. Wash your own hands first, quietly saying, "As I wash my hands, I'm washing away anger and worry." Then direct your children to place their hands over the bowl, one by one. Pour the water over their hands and encourage them to imagine washing negative feelings away with the dirt. Tell them to enter the dining room and seat themselves quietly.

Where does our food come from?

Does your dinner-time question "What did you do at school today?" routinely produce the answer "Nothing" (or, as my older daughter says with increasing frequency, "I don't want to talk about it")?

To spark thought-provoking dinner conversation, encourage your children to consider what they are eating and how it came to your table. Considering the many people and animals whose efforts have contributed to putting food on your table teaches children about the interdependence of all living things. Engage your children in conversation with a few simple questions posed while preparing or sharing a meal.

Discuss the global origins of your meal's dishes and ingredients: spaghetti from China via Italy, potatoes from South America, black pepper from India, and so on. Point out that until recent advances in refrigeration and transportation, people could only eat foods from their own immediate area.

Talk about what part of a plant each vegetable on the table represents: root, stem, leaf, flower, fruit, seed... Point out that without insects these plants could never produce fruit and seeds. If you eat dairy, eggs, or meat, discuss what kind of animals they come from and what it meant to the animal to provide this food for you. Encourage the children to consider all the different people involved in bringing this food to your table: farm workers, truckers, grocery store workers, and so on.

THINGS TO DO

Create a family tradition dish

My children and I have a favorite dish—an Oriental salad made with noodles—that we like to bring to school and family gatherings. Whenever we make this dish, each daughter claims her favorite step as her responsibility. One crushes the block of dried noodles, the other helps prepare the dressing. I always get a warm feeling that we are creating a family tradition as well as a memory that will last for many years. You and your kids can develop some of your own healthy recipes that you prepare together. In *The Kopan Cookbook: Vegetarian Recipes from a Tibetan Monastery*, author Betty Jung includes authentic recipes she collected during a year spent assisting the head cook in a Buddhist monastery in Nepal. Your kids are sure to love the following fried cheese snack:

Cheese stick pakoras

8 ounces hard white mild cheese (Swiss)

⅔ cup white flour

¼ tsp baking powder

½ tsp salt

¼ tsp ground black pepper

1 egg

½ cup water

Pinch of Indian Tomato Red Powder (optional)

Oil for deep frying

Cut cheese into bite-size sticks, approximately 3 inches long by ½ inch wide. Mix all dry ingredients in a small bowl. Add egg and water. Mix well with a wire whisk. Dip cheese stick in batter until well-coated. Heat oil in wok or frying pan over medium heat. When oil is hot, add coated cheese sticks one by one. Lower heat and cook for 2-3 minutes or until cheese begins to bubble and ooze through the coating. Remove and drain on paper towels; serve hot.

The television is sometimes an intrusive guest at family meals. Thich Nhat Hanh, in an essay entitled "Practicing Mindfulness at Meals," recommends turning off the TV and simply enjoying being with one another. He suggests that those taking a meal together breathe in and out three times before they eat. "Talking, laughing, and smiling in the kitchen together is a very wonderful thing" (Eastoak, 229). Cleaning up afterward is an essential part of a Zen meal. At the very least, kids should scrape off their own plates and bowls and put them in the sink or dishwasher before skipping off to their next activity.

A Buddhist food blessing

The Tibetan food blessing is a way to remember the kindness of the three jewels of Buddhism: Buddha, Dharma, and Sangha. The food you eat is considered an offering to the jewels. In order to make a proper offering, the food should first be blessed. As you bless the food, visualize that your plate is multiplied limitless times until it fills the whole universe.

Om Ah Hum (3x)
I and my circle, throughout all of our lives,
May we never be separated from the protection of the
Three Precious Jewels.
By continuously making offering to the Three
Precious Jewels, may their blessings be obtained.
Buddha, the peerless Master,
Dharma, the peerless Protector,
Sangha, the peerless Helper.
We make these offerings to the three precious
Protectors.
Om Ah Hum

This prayer is a little longer than others. If you say it quietly to yourself as others are saying their Christian prayers, you will be going on after they are already done. There are other, shorter blessings you can say, such as this prayer that comes from the Zen Buddhist tradition, which emphasizes awakening to the present moment through seated meditation:

I take this food to stop all evil,
to practice good,
and to accomplish the Buddha way.

The important thing is not the exact prayer, but that your children learn to give thanks for their meal and all that went into creating and providing it. The Buddhist aspect of the food blessing is to visualize the food being transformed within into positive energy that can be used to help other beings.
You might also recite the Precepts for Young People, which author Sandy Eastoak describes as the Three Pure Precepts. They are the basis for all other moral teachings:

- *Do no harm*
- *Do only good*
- *Do good for others*

Encouraging children to share and take turns

Children naturally offer things to one another. When you watch kids at play you'll find it truly beautiful to see how they invent imaginary worlds and exchange action figures, marbles, or other toys without a second thought. Encourage the quality of generosity that already exists within your children when they play with their friends. They will find it easier to share with children they don't know and with adults as well. Sharing is a way of experiencing the joy of thinking of someone else and recognizing their needs. Sometimes it is a matter of seeing the love and kindness that exists naturally in your children and giving those qualities the space to blossom. Consider creating situations that foster generosity, such as:

- **Caring for pets.** Involve your children in feeding, cleaning, and grooming as soon as a pet enters the household.
- **Caring for dolls and other toys.** Younger children who play with dolls and other figures should be encouraged to put them to "bed" nicely in an orderly home (such as a box) when it is not playtime, and to "feed" and dress them nicely when it is.

Of course, in order for children to learn patience, they need to have an example of it themselves. Where else are they going to learn it? According to Jacqueline Mandell, "Much of children's learning happens in a non-linear way. Since our children use repetition to explore their world, this requires great patience." Patience requires us to:

- Accept the present moment as it is
- Be flexible and calm
- Foster perseverance of inquiry without expectations or time constraints
- Rejoice in our children's small and great discoveries
- Respect the timelessness of children's play (Eastoak, 260)

What to say when you hear "I'm bored!"

Two of the most dreaded words my children can utter aren't "I'm sick" but, rather, "I'm bored." If my girls fall ill, I know I have to care for them by feeding them soup or wrapping them up on the couch and urging them to get some rest. At such moments, my job is obvious.

When I hear "I'm bored," my first impulse is to react as though the kids are ill. If I am not mindful, I will hurry to them and suggest ways to relieve this state. I feel as though I have to care for the kids and provide them with amusements or, at the very least, suggestions of how to fill up their time. Often, I find myself suggesting the very things that I oppose at other times: "Play a computer game or put on a movie to watch."

Sitting with dissatisfaction

What does "I'm bored" really mean? Does it mean "I want attention" or "I want to play with you" or "I want to find someone to play with?" Sometimes boredom isn't exactly what it means. Encourage your child to sit with this feeling quietly for a moment. If you have a space available for meditation, contemplation, or reading, encourage her to sit there. Or she can just look out the window and think about it. It may be that she is avoiding a homework assignment. Or perhaps she is feeling sad because one of her friends has decided to play with someone else. A walking meditation around the block or around the garden or in the woods might help. She is certain to find bugs, butterflies, or wildlife to interest her. My daughter can't always put her feelings into words, but if I put a hunk of clay in her hands, she will work on it for an hour, creating something beautiful. Somehow this works out whatever angst she is experiencing in a way that words cannot address.

Embracing daily distractions

If life were quiet and peaceful all the time, there would be no need to grow. We would be relaxed and meditative as a matter of course. We would also have no occasion to share our spiritual progress with other beings. Luckily for us, we aren't handicapped by a constant state of peace and quiet. We have reasons to strive, to seek peace and calm almost hungrily, whether through the formal practice of meditation or by simply being mindful and calm in the midst of our busy lives. As parents, there is little we can do to escape the demands of raising children: keeping house, paying bills, helping with homework, and acting as chauffeur. Nor should we try to escape them. Just as His Holiness the Dalai Lama instructs spiritual practitioners to embrace their enemies and be grateful to those enemies for spurring them on to spiritual progress, so too we should rejoice that we are tired and stressed

His Holiness the Dalai Lama

The Dalai Lama is the spiritual leader of the Tibetan people and of several Buddhist sects that once flourished in Tibet. The current Dalai Lama, who was born in 1935 with the name Lhamo Dhondrub and is now known as Tenzin Gyatso, is revered not only by Tibetans but by Buddhists and others around the world. In his life, the Dalai Lama has faced great adversity. In 1959, he was forced to flee Tibet when the country was invaded by the Chinese. He lives in exile in Dharmsala, India, and travels the world teaching and speaking out on behalf of Tibetan independence. Your children might be inspired by reading his life story in his book *My Land and My People: The Original Autobiography of His Holiness the Dalai Lama* (New York: Warner Books, 1987), or by watching the movie *Kundun*.

out and have so many things to do. Our children will teach us to be calm in any situation. And, thanks to impermanence, it will all be over before we know it and they will be off on their own. So let's embrace the stress and chaos of parenting while we can, and use it to move forward on the spiritual path.

Embracing chaos as path

Illusions allow us to get through our daily activities. If we didn't have the illusion that we are safe while driving in our cars, we would probably never go out on the city streets. If we didn't hold on to the illusion that we are going to live forever, that we are going to have many other chances to patch things up with estranged relatives or complete projects that we have been dreaming about for years, we would probably never go to work at all.

One of the illusions we hold dear is the notion that, as parents, we are in control of what happens in our domain—our household. Here, at least, we can set a schedule and stick to it; we can lay down rules of behavior that our children and their playmates will observe. The young people in the house will come when summoned, the table will be cleared when we order it done ... By now, you can see how much of this is just fantasy.

The problem occurs when the young people shatter our illusions by creating a mess, failing to come when summoned, or neglecting to clean up before a meal, yet we cling to our fantasy and feel a rush of helpless rage. You may find yourself ranting, "How dare they ignore me! Why doesn't everyone listen to me?"

In an article entitled "Cartoon as Path," Lama John Makransky tells an excellent story about coming home exhausted, hungry, and stressed out from work (Makransky, 122). Instead of being greeted by a happy household, he finds a tense atmosphere in which children are bickering, his wife is cranky and ignored by the kids, and no one even notices him. He feels a rush of rage and "a wish to take complete control, to make home the welcoming place it was *supposed* to be on my arrival." He then uses a special mind–heart training that involves the exchange of loving kindness. This enables him to turn his rage and lack of control into a moment of spiritual realization. I have adapted the steps in the following exercise.

Exchange your rage

No one said parenting was easy. You're going to feel angry and unhappy, whether it's with yourself, your external circumstances, your spouse or ex-spouse, or with your kids. Catch yourself when you are angry and practice exchanging your feeling for the pain and anger countless other beings are going through as well. With practice, you will be able to recognize your anger, feel it, and work through it before you open your mouth and express it.

1. Feel your rage, anger, desire to control, impatience, and stress as fully as possible. Simply experience it without screaming or reacting. Imagine how it would feel for someone else to experience the same feelings.

2. When you are fully immersed in the feeling, think: "This is what countless people are experiencing!" In the midst of your own pain, your own impatience, realize that you are experiencing the difficulties that many other beings are undergoing at this very moment.

3. Take the feelings of your own and everyone else's distraction, stress, overload, worry, and lack of control into your heart. Imagine that you are removing these feelings from everyone else. The pressure, the weight of all that emotion, opens your heart and allows radiant compassion to flow throughout all the parts of

your body. It then radiates forth to all others who are undergoing the same discomfort.

4. Let your mind and body relax. Be calm. Feel that space has opened so you can accept the chaos of family life with humor; appreciate how absorbed your kids are in their own selves and their friends; realize the beauty of the moment (even when they are bickering), and rejoice that you are all together and healthy.

Now you can speak to your children calmly and guide them without a trace of anger or stress to what they need to do.

This exercise might seem complex, but with practice you might be able to squeeze it into a matter of seconds. You might feel a compressed version:

1. Feel the pain
2. Everyone has the same pain
3. Take on their pain; give back love
4. Relax; embrace the moment

If you can do even part of this exercise between the time your kids make you feel angry and impatient and the time you react, you'll all be better off for it. As Jack Kornfield says, "Parenting is a labor of love. It's a path of service and surrender and, like the practice of a Buddha or Bodhisattva (a seeker of enlightenment), it demands patience, understanding and tremendous sacrifice. It is also a way to reconnect with the mystery of life" (Rosman, 9).

Fully focus on your children

There will never be more worthy recipients of your total attention than your children, yet it's easy to take them for granted. Perhaps you see them at the same time every day. Perhaps they become associated in your mind with this or that task—picking them up from school, taking them to a music lesson. You may not look at them or pay attention to them when you are wrapped up in your usual worries and preoccupations. Then one day you see your son or daughter walk onstage at the school holiday show and you are astonished: "Is that my daughter? When did she get to be so tall?"

Many of the most beautiful moments of parenting may be ones we do not fully experience. We may be unable to fully appreciate the fact that our children are happy, that your daughter said something hilarious, or that your son created something beautiful. Why? Because we are busy worrying about the weather, the traffic, a pending work deadline, or any number of other distractions. We need to develop the ability to lift the veil, put aside our daily problems, and be truly present, both for ourselves and for our children.

You can develop your ability to focus attention on your children by practicing concentration on a task. Many Buddhists keep a home altar for worship and spiritual practice. If you have an altar, you can focus your attention by dusting the altar mindfully. You don't need an altar for this activity, though: a mantel or bureau topped with objects important to you will also work well.

Choose two cloths. Admire their weave and their color. Notice the texture of the fabric. Dampen one in water, paying particular attention to the sound and feel of the water coming from the tap. Smell each of them, noting their similarities and differences. Then pick up each object on your altar, one at a time. As you wipe first with the damp cloth and then with the dry cloth, note the angles or curves of each object. Enjoy the way the light creates shadows and causes colors to come to life. Block everything else from your mind and focus only on what each instant brings to your consciousness in the way of sight, sound, smell, and touch.

Later, you can begin to apply some of these techniques to interactions with your child. You see him all the time, but pretend it is your first meeting. Try to find something you've never noticed before, such as a wisp of hair on his forehead or a freckle on his chin. When you care enough to be fully present with him, he will in turn feel loved just as he is. Regular practice during normal, everyday times will pay off during stressful moments when he needs to know that you are there for him with your wholehearted attention. Because it is natural to zero in on your child when he is misbehaving, it is important to be intentional with special time when he is being good.

Listen and reflect back

Carl Rogers developed client-centered psychotherapy, which taught practitioners how to truly listen to people. It's an activity that is practiced all too seldom. Whether you're talking to a friend, interacting at a Buddhist retreat, or finding out from your son how his day went, make an effort to listen first and ask questions later. You don't necessarily have to agree with everything that's being said, but it's very important to respect the person (no matter how small) who is speaking. All too often, parents respond to a complaint or request by snapping or immediately prescribing a solution for a problem. It takes patience to become a good listener by avoiding the urge to make snap judgments. Try the following:

1. When your son (or daughter) is talking to you, take a deep breath. Clear your mind as much as possible and listen to what he is saying.

2. Say "Uh-huh" or "I see" to indicate to your child that you are listening closely. Kids have a tendency to shuffle back and forth or walk around aimlessly when trying to convey something important. It is often physically difficult for them to get the words out. Your son or daughter may not look you in the eyes or acknowledge that you are listening, so encourage him or her to go on, without interrupting or making judgments.

3. Here's the tricky part. When your child is through making a statement, he or she will pause. Your impulse will be to make a judgment about the situation or to provide instructions on what to do. Resist this temptation. Instead, reflect back exactly what you have been told. For example:

- Your child says: "I told Melanie that I wanted to be by myself and do my studying, and like, she sat down like I didn't say anything and she just started talking to me and she took out her books right there at the table."
- Your usual response: "You should have just told her to leave you alone" or "What's wrong with having a friend want to be with you?"
- Better, reflective response: "You told her you wanted to be alone but she just sat down anyway and ignored what you said."

4. Let your child continue. He will add more details or come to logical conclusions, encouraged by knowing that you are listening and not making judgments.

You'll be gratified by the response you get. Rather than getting in an argument with your child or hearing the dreaded phrase, "You're not listening to me!" you'll see your child feel better. You may not solve the problem. Or your child may ask you for advice, and then take it. You may also get a hug for your listening efforts. And you'll get the best payoff, which is seeing your child's distress fade and some measure (or at least hint) of contentment return.

Practices make perfect: creating a sacred space

Everyone needs a refuge, and your children are no exception. The construction of a meditation and worship space in your house not only makes your spiritual beliefs visible to your children but also provides a way for them to participate with you, even if they choose not to meditate or practice.

THINGS TO DO

Create a cabinet shrine

Whether you are a Buddhist or not, you do not need to prominently display all the symbols of your beliefs. Your home should be as welcoming as any other. Some Buddhists don't have a meditation room as such; rather, they keep their Buddhist shrine (an enclosed space containing objects of prayer or worship) in a cabinet. The doors of the cabinet are closed or opened as needed. When non-Buddhists or guests who would not be receptive to the practice visit the home, the cabinet doors are closed. If a gathering of Buddhists is held, or when the residents of the house prepare to perform their daily prayers, the doors are opened. A friend of mine follows the Nichiren Buddhism tradition (a form of Buddhism developed by the monk Nichiren in Japan in the 13th century). She keeps her shrine in her dining room and sits on a chair before it for a period of time each day as she does her daily practice. Another friend, a Tibetan Buddhist follower, has a meditation room as well as a cabinet shrine. When Buddhist guests come to call, his son opens the cabinet; when non-Buddhists visit, his son closes it.

Pick a small cabinet for this purpose—perhaps a foot in width by two feet in height, or whatever fits your available space. If you can, find a cabinet with two doors that fold out, from the center, like wings opening up. This style is more aesthetically pleasing than one with a single door that folds out. You'll find a beautiful example on the Wood Arts Education Alliance website at *http://www.woodworkersguild. com/artisan.asp?ID=10&name=Bill+Light*. Be sure you have enough space inside for a representation of the Buddha, a set of seven offering bowls (bowls that contain clear water used as offerings—or one bowl, if you lack the space), incense, and perhaps some dried flowers.

THINGS TO DO

Creating a home altar

Most Buddhists designate some area within their
home as a meditation space—a place where people
can be quiet and contemplative and enjoy privacy if
they need it. In fact, everyone needs such a space,
whether they consider themselves Buddhist or not.
Do you have one room in the house that isn't filled
with toys, clothes, books, or other clutter? If you
can't spare an entire room, designate part of a room. If
you don't have any room indoors, set up a sacred
space in your yard. The area should be kept tidy so
that your practice will be clean and positive, and so
you and your children can show respect and value for
the dharma.

An altar is a central place of worship for many
Buddhists. In contrast to a shrine, which takes the
form of a cabinet or other small, enclosed space, an
altar is a larger flat surface such as a table. It's also a
great way to get your children involved with your
practice. After all, they love to construct things.
While they are helping you with cleaning and gathering pillows, tell them a little bit about what you are
doing:

• The altar is an important place to think about the
  kindness and compassion of the Buddha and the
  other enlightened beings.

- The altar is the place where you invite the Buddha and the enlightened spirits to help you.
- The substances you offer on the altar include water, light in the form of candles, incense, and flowers. Gather photos of important people in your family and your immediate circle of friends and place them on your altar.

Whether you set aside a meditation area or create an altar for making offerings, it's important to maintain an open-door policy. When you are meditating or saying your daily prayers, leave your door slightly ajar so that your children don't feel you have left them or that they cannot disturb you. If they barge in and jump on your lap or even try to take some bowls from your altar, rejoice that they have given you such a good opportunity to practice patience. Try not to be the sort of practitioner who visualizes love and compassion for all beings while on the cushion but, the moment someone bumps the cushion, instantly becomes enraged so all positive energy flies out the window.

Daily chores and cleaning

Buddhism is an eminently practical spiritual path. Finding pleasure in the ordinary is an essential aspect of Buddhist practice. Does that mean you don't instruct your kids to do chores? Of course not. Tell them what to do—but with compassion and kindness. The dinner table, laundry room, and kitchen can all be places that facilitate spiritual growth. One activity that links all of these household centers is cleaning.

Like any spiritual activity, cleaning can be an empty chore that you simply move through mechanically in order to get to the next task, or it can be imbued with significance. In terms of Buddhist spirituality, cleaning is the first of the six preliminaries to one's daily prayers and practices. In order to place your cushion and set up your altar, you need to clear a physical space. More importantly, being in a clean area will make you feel good, and being clear of negativities such as anxiety or dissatisfaction about the state of your surroundings will improve your practice.

As you clean, you can tell yourself that you are becoming more patient and more appreciative of your family and your home. If you place your own anger, attachment, and ignorance in the trash along with the dust, you are bound to have a fuller store of resources for parenting, and that will have an indirect but important impact on your children. If they see you humming and smiling as you sweep and scrub and put things away, and if they see how happy you are after you clean, they'll also feel better about themselves. They may begin to think, "Maybe there's something to this Buddhist stuff after all."

On a deeper level, cleaning has to do with purification: the process of clearing obstacles and negativities to one's spiritual progress. The Buddha recommended the act of cleaning as the most important practice for purification. As you clean, visualize that you are cleaning away your delusions. Children can certainly get more out of cleaning their rooms than just the satisfaction of their parents. Encourage them to pay attention to their feelings after the cleaning is done; they will probably agree that it feels better to be in a clean room rather than a disorderly one.

DISCUSSION STARTER

Did the Buddha have to clean his room?

The points of discussion listed below can come in handy whether you encounter opposition to cleaning or receptivity to learning the role of cleaning in one's Buddhist practice.

Q. Did the Buddha complain about having to share his stuff?

Q. What did the Buddha do when his little sister kept nagging him about playing with his toys and ended up breaking them?

Q. Did the Buddha ever just want to go to his room and be alone?

Q. What did the Buddha do when his mom and dad were arguing?

Q. Why do I feel like no one listens to me or understands me at home?

These are all questions that fall under the heading "What would Buddha do?" You don't have to answer them literally. After all, your son or daughter is growing up in a very different time and facing different circumstances than the Buddha (or Christ, or Mohammed) did. But these discussion starters are all about different ways to approach life and life's challenges. Yes, Buddha cleaned his room; yes, Buddha probably did share his toys. But he may have felt alone at times, and he may have felt discouraged. The point is that it's okay to feel your own feelings. The trick is to not get attached to those feelings for long periods of time, but be receptive to the new feelings that inevitably arise to replace them. Your child might feel resistant to cleaning or sharing, and may want to be alone. But encourage your children to think through their feelings and sit with them for a while, then try a more enlightened approach. After sulking and complaining, think about some way to share that wouldn't be so painful. Perhaps working out an exchange, or sharing one thing instead of two or three, would help, for instance. Perhaps writing a poem, drawing a picture, or playing the piano would help work through moments of anxiety or distress. Be patient, let your kids work through their feelings, and help them feel they are not alone.

THINGS TO DO

Sweep away your anger, throw away your attachment

Buy a miniature broom and dustpan for your children and, as they sweep, tell them the story of the monk who, as he swept, cleared away his delusions and eventually became enlightened. In other words, he came to learn the true nature of existence and gained limitless compassion for all beings. Encourage your children to clear away any debris they find on the floor of your home. Encourage them to make believe that such things are feelings that are holding them back, such as jealousy, longing for something, or anger. You don't have to use terms like "compassion" and "delusions," but substitute terms such as "bad feelings" and "good feelings," for instance. If they are unhappy or angry with someone, ask them to imagine that they are clearing away their anger or other unpleasant feelings along with the dirt.

When the room is clean, stand with your child and rejoice, then ask, "Do you feel different now? Do you feel less angry?" Simply walking away from the room would make the cleaning seem merely a task done to fulfill their parents' instructions. Stopping to rejoice and noticing how different the cleaning makes one feel gives the act significance. If you want to take the process a step further, you and your child can make a wish that the cleaning will bring good things to all beings.

STORIES TO READ ALOUD

The story of Lam Chung

There was once a wealthy Brahmin family living in India during the Buddha's lifetime. They tried to raise a number of children, but those children did not survive. When they had another child, they took the child to a wise woman who was able to tell fortunes to ask how they could enable the child to survive. The wise woman put a bit of butter in the child's mouth and told the maidservant who brought the child to take it out into a busy main road and ask anyone who passed by to pray for the child. Many great teachers went by and told the maidservant they would pray for the child. The child survived and was given the name Lam Chen, which means "Great Road."

A younger son was born to the family, and the maidservant did the same thing with the little boy. But she took this child to a small, less-traveled road and nobody passed by. Then the Buddha came along. When the maidservant approached and asked the Buddha to pray for the child, he said, "May this child survive, may he live, join my order, and achieve ultimate enlightenment—the ultimate realization of what's important in the world." The child was given the name Lam Chung, "Small Road."

The older brother proved to be very intelligent and studied in many different schools, becoming a very wise student of the Buddha. The younger brother was not at all smart. He was kicked out of every school he tried to get into. His older brother tried to help him but could not.

Lam Chung was sitting against a stone walk, crying in despair, when Buddha came along. Buddha told him to come with him. The Buddha knew the boy couldn't learn anything through reading or studying. Buddha gave him the job of cleaning. First, he cleaned the shoes of everyone in the sangha-monastery where the Buddha was living. He was taught to memorize, as he cleaned, the phrase "Clean the dust, clean the dirt." After he learned this, he was given the job of sweeping up the temple. After he swept one side, Buddha caused dust to be raised on the other side. As a result, he had to move back and forth, cleaning, for a long time. One day he wondered to himself, "Why do I keep saying 'Clean the dust, clean the dirt'? What does it mean?" Suddenly, he realized: "This dirt is the thing I keep thinking about all the time. I keep looking at this dirt and doing this sweeping, and I never do anything else. I'm attached to it. It's keeping me caught up in the present so I can't understand what's really important." He said:

> *This dust is not ordinary dust,*
> *It is the dust of attachment.*
> *And if you are intelligent*
> *You should be able to remove that from you.*
>
> *This dirt is not ordinary dirt,*
> *This is the dirt of anger.*
> *And if you are intelligent*
> *You should be able to remove that from you.*
> (Rimpoche, 76–7)

By sweeping the floor as his only practice, he was able to learn something truly important. He went on to learn much more and eventually became a very well-known and popular Buddhist teacher.

Helping your child deal with mass culture

Children are bombarded by many influences that run counter to everything the Buddha taught. Popular movies, TV, and computer games teach them about violence and overconsumption. These pastimes also rob families of time together.

It's not necessary to be against all computer games and video amusements, of course. The Mahayana path teaches that it's all a matter of balance. Choose what your children can play and set a schedule during which it's all right to play. Rather than having them play in isolation, ask questions about their games and even join in the game yourself.

Be a conscious TV watcher

My own guru (the Buddhist term for teacher) watches television, especially when it comes to news networks. He also watches movies, both on television and in the theater. I am sure he sometimes watches such shows passively, the way we all do. But there is one big difference between the way he takes in visual media and the way most people do: he is always learning. He is constantly on the lookout for symbols and analogies that he can use to better convey his teachings to Western students.

Those of us who know him well are familiar with his references to enlightening movies. (One of his favorites is called *The Neverending Story*.) He will even mention commercials for products, for instance, if he is comparing people who cannot curb their insatiable desires to the dog that obsessively craves a particular dog food.

Just as the guru teaches "Drive the car, don't let the car drive you," remember to control the TV; don't let the TV control you or your kids. Turn your passive viewing into a more active project. You, too, can be on the lookout for analogies that your children will understand. Watch TV with them and, when something violent takes place, point out that it's not real. If someone on the program steals something, you can begin a spiritual or moral discussion about it.

DISCUSSION STARTER

The judo flip

How many times have you seen it: your children watch a martial arts saga or other violent movie. Afterward, they engage in violent activity themselves, no matter how briefly. Encourage them to stop and be mindful. Instead of saying, "Don't push your brother," get in the habit of saying, "What were you thinking about when you pushed your brother?" This takes the focus off the action and puts it on the cause; the state of mind that gives rise to violent action. Call attention to your kids' state of mind in a non-threatening way, for example, by talking about your own state of mind: "I feel nervous and agitated after watching that movie. What a strange feeling. Do you feel that way, too?"

Judo and Buddhism

Martial arts such as judo and aikido teach practitioners how to deflect someone else's negative energy: if someone attacks you, you learn to evade them, flip them over, and throw them to the ground, thus neutralizing their negativity. Often, Buddhist meditations seem to flip around conventional conceptions and present them from a completely new perspective. The people we see as "enemies" are helping us to grow and progress. When we become too attached to someone, we can visualize her growing old and withered, which helps to lessen the attachment. In the same way, movies, television shows, and video games are not all bad. Use them as tools to teach your children how to schedule their activities, how to walk away from them when they are over, and to emphasize that the things they see are make-believe and not an example to be followed.

THINGS TO DO

Observe "Turn off the TV" week

Many families only watch television at certain times, perhaps on special occasions or when they are all together. Other families don't watch television at all. Turning off the TV can dramatically change a child's perspective. Schedule a "Turn off the TV" week once a year or a "Turn off the TV" day once a month. During that time, try to spend as much time as you can with your children, focusing on reading or enjoying the great outdoors.

The act of turning the TV off is a moment of spiritual cleansing. Instantly, the images and distractions that seemed all too vivid just a few seconds ago have vanished. The Buddha spoke of building sand castles in the same way:

> Just as when, Radha, boys and girls play with
> little sand-castles, so long as they are not rid
> of lust, not rid of desire, not rid of affection,
> thirst, feverish longing and craving for those
> little sand-castles, just so long as they do
> delight in them, are amused by them, set store
> of them, are jealous of them.
>
> But, Radha, as soon as those boys and girls are
> rid of lust, of desire and affection, are rid of
> thirst, feverish longing, and craving for those
> little sand-castles, straightaway with hand and
> foot they scatter them, break them up, knock
> them down, cease to play with them.
> (Woodward, 218)

Children are good at abandoning one thing and moving on to the next. (They are especially good, as I'm sure you have noticed, at moving on without picking up after themselves.) Take advantage of this natural talent and encourage them to move on from a disappointment to something more fruitful, or from a movie or TV show to something more worthwhile, such as reading a book.

Balance televised images with spiritual designs

Images are powerful. If you don't believe me, just ask someone in marketing or public relations. Even if you try to limit the time your children spend in front of the television, they are visually assaulted by billboards on the highway and, if they take the bus, by posters above the seats. It is rare for one of these photos or drawings in a Western country to have a Buddhist motif, yet there are many Buddhist images that are beautiful to admire and meaningful to discuss. How can you make Buddhist imagery part of your child's experience? The Wheel of Life is eye-catching because it depicts a big monster, Yama, holding up the entire universe. There are also some vivid depictions of the six hell realms that are sure to hold your children's attention. (The hell realms are regions where a being can go after death, if they accumulate a great deal of negative energy/negative karma; some hell realms are hot, some cold; in some beings experience great hunger, and in some beings experience terrible pain.) Your children will be interested in virtually any mandala. Kids love castles and elaborate constructions. They will appreciate the structure of the mandala when you point out the wisdom fire around the edge, the cemeteries, the four gates leading into the structure, and the important deities in the center. The Dalai Lama himself explains the meaning of the Wheel of Time mandala to children, and the meaning of the Kalachakra teaching and initiation ceremony, in *Learning from the Dalai Lama: Secrets of the Wheel of Time*, by Karen Pandell and Barry Bryant (Dutton Books, 1995).

Shield your child from video-game overload

You can't completely shield your children from computers and other electronic games. If they are banned in your household, they may well be present in the homes of your children's friends. The problem is not necessarily in playing the games, but in learning to stop playing after a certain time. It can be helpful to set a time limit, particularly when the kids disagree over who plays when. You can set an egg timer or alarm clock to go off after 30 minutes of play. Learning to turn games off and walk away is good practice for kids.

The Buddha wasn't talking about video games when he made the following statements, but they can be applied to many forms of stimulation that produce attachment and dissatisfaction in young people:

> Then that child, following his growth, following the
> ripening of his faculties, now roams about possessed of,
> equipped with the five pleasures of sense, [and susceptible
> to] forms [that can be perceived] by eye, ear, nose,
> tongue, and tangible by body, all of them longed for,
> alluring, delightful, dear, inviting to sensual delight...
> Seeing a shape with the eye, he is enamored of enticing
> shapes, is repelled by repellent shapes, and dwells with
> mindfulness not established and has but little
> thought...Thus he comes to know satisfaction, and dissat-
> isfactions: whatever feeling he feels, be it pleasant,

*painful, or neutral, he welcomes it, greets it, and clings
fast to it.* (Woodward, 29)

One wonders what a constant sense of dissatisfaction and a constant desire to gratify do to a child. With a continual wish to do something else or see something else, how well can he or she concentrate on homework, or how much mental attention can he or she have to devote to other beings?

THINGS TO DO

Assemble a treasure box

After the TV and the video games are turned off, you may be left wondering what to do with your child. Not only may he be used to switching on the electronic amusement at certain times, but you, too, may be accustomed to having a few minutes to yourself while he is watching the screen. Prepare for such moments by creating a "treasure box"—a drawer in a desk or cupboard where items that you and your children have collected over a period of time are stored. Here are suggestions for what to collect and what to do with each item:

- **Collect items from nature as well as indoors.** This brings in the outside world even when you're confined due to cold or bad weather.

- **Give each item a name.** Names are important because they make us pay closer attention to objects we might overlook otherwise.
- **Include some spiritual items.** These might include statues, prayer cards, or other trinkets. You can discuss these items and their relevance with your children.

You can buy Buddhist or other spiritually related items over the Internet or at museum stores, but be sure to keep your eyes open at resale shops and garage sales. Plenty of treasures come to the surface that would be perfect for your purpose. Before putting an item in your box, work with your child to create an index card describing it, or write a poem or draw a picture about it. You can also make up riddles for your child to solve. In any case, your kids will have plenty of fun matching the index card to the item (set a timer to see how fast this can be done) or make a new game for your child's next play-date.

Introduce the concept of spiritual community to your children

The Buddhist concept of sangha, a group of spiritual practitioners who help one another along the path, is beneficial for children in many ways. If your children see you interacting with your own spiritual community, they learn how important your beliefs are to you. If you belong to a community that welcomes children and gives them the means to interact with one another, by all means take advantage of it. Even if you only attend one or two yearly retreats at which children are allowed, this is a great way to make your kids aware of the wider spiritual world to which you—and they—belong.

On an everyday basis, it's important to reach out to the community in your own neighborhood. Developing a network of parents in your neighborhood or at your school not only provides playmates for your children, but also gives you a chance to care for other kids and exchange transportation, meals, and other duties in a cooperative way. The notion that friends exist all around and that groups of people can help one another can extend, in a child's flexible and expansive mind, to the whole world.

Sponsor a child

When my own children were aged seven and nine years old, we had the opportunity to sponsor a ten-year-old Tibetan child who fled to India to attend a school for refugees. This opened up a new level of awareness for my children, who not only had a new "sister" (the girl adopted me as a second father and my daughters as her sisters) but also a connection to someone far away who needed assistance.

Ideally, your motivation should be for all other beings. Children naturally want all beings to be happy and at peace. They can easily become concerned and worried about wars and other world conflicts. If they hear about a war in another part of the world, they may express fear that they will be bombed or killed. Make your home a refuge and place of safety. At the same time, make them aware that all beings are interconnected and things they can do at home will help others who live in faraway lands.

THINGS TO DO

Promote citizenship

One simple and useful way to promote being a good citizen and a member of a wider community is to know who your elected officials are. Do *you* know who all of your government representatives are? Draw up a list of all the public officials who represent you in the government, along with their contact information, and keep it handy so you can refer to it if an issue arises (or if your child asks you about it).

Here's another suggestion: be a good neighbor. Bake some cookies and give them out to your neighbors. Clean up any papers or other litter you find on your block. Also make an effort to keep the school grounds clean. If your children see you caring for property that technically doesn't belong to you, it conveys a powerful message of interdependence. It tells them that they need to be responsible for their whole community, not just their individual household.

PART TWO

School, friendships, and feelings

Buddhism can provide practical ways for kids to cope with tests, teasing, homework, and other school-related challenges. The Buddhist virtues of patience and enthusiasm (which are, of course, integral to many other religions) can help kids learn to see every experience—even a math test or a gym class—as a positive learning opportunity.

School is a microcosm of the challenges a child will face growing up. These challenges are magnified by the closed community and established curriculum. Outside of school, kids can (or at least *believe* they can) do anything they want. Once they get into school, they lose that control. They are shuttled from class to class, from lunch to gymnasium, often with no time to spare. They are taught subjects that don't immediately seem relevant to their daily experience—after all, how can algebra or world geography be applied to kicking a soccer ball or romping with the family dog in the park?

Then there are the social interactions associated with school. Often, the friendships that develop during our school years last a lifetime. On the other hand, negative interactions with other peers can lead to low self-esteem, jealousy, bickering, and bullying. These wounds also can last a lifetime. Whether your child is the one left out or the one deciding that someone else is "not cool," supportive parenting is vital to developing healthy and responsible social skills. Sharing your Buddhist beliefs and practices can help your children integrate into their own community while not alienating them from their peers.

Enthusiasm and homework do mix

You probably hear it the moment the kids come home: "Why do we have to do homework? Can't we play first?" If your kids are like mine, they'll use every trick in the book in an attempt to avoid doing their assignments. I've heard: "I'll do it while my sister is at her violin lesson," "It's not due until next week," and my favorite: "It's so easy, I can do it in a couple of minutes—I'll get to it later."

I wish my daughters would enjoy doing their homework and look on it as a positive activity. But no matter how much I try to impress on them the importance of homework to their overall learning experience, my words don't seem to have an effect unless they are backed up by routine. Here, my daily Buddhist practice has helped me to create a homework ritual you might want to try yourself.

EXERCISE

Creating a homework ritual

Ritual is an important part of Buddhist practice. Think about your own daily prayers, moments of silence, moments of thanks, or periods of meditation. You can do them anywhere, but they have greater impact if you do them in the same time and in the same place, using the same ritual objects. Objects such as a meditation cushion, prayer book, and special cloth to place under the prayer book give your prayers more meaning. Doing your prayers at the same time every day helps you remember to do them all.

In fact, I get so consumed by work and kids that the only way to ensure enough time for my daily practice is to know that it will be done in exactly the same time and place—at the end of the day, just before I go to bed. I have also established a routine of doing some morning prayers while behind the wheel of my car.

In a similar way, you can encourage your kids to do their homework willingly by establishing a homework ritual. Come up with an official time period that your children recognize as "homework time" and a special place where they can do their work. Creating this ritual can turn homework into a sort of spiritual practice for children (though I wouldn't call it that; they may rebel if you invest it with too much importance). Here are some suggestions:

- Have your kids do homework at the same time every day. For me, this is immediately after they return from school. Right after dinner can also work well.
- Establish a signal that announces the start of homework time. You can ring a bell (or strike the side of a "singing bowl" if you have one) or do what I do: Announce the words "Homework time!" while you are putting your coats and bags away.
- Suggest that they take a moment to remember their

real motivation for doing their homework: not just to get an *A*, not just to prevent their teacher from being unhappy, but to learn something and to become a better person so they can go on to help other people. In the beginning, you'll need to recite this concept (or a condensed version) a few times. Eventually, you'll be able to simply say, "Check your motivation," and they'll know what you mean.

- Cover the table or desk with a special cloth that is used only for homework.

- Provide special workspaces where the children can do their work. They may sit wherever they want, but you can arrange a variety of tables, chairs, and nooks so they have options from which to choose.

- When homework is done, praise your children and suggest they make a wish that their efforts might contribute to the well-being of everyone else.

STORIES TO READ ALOUD

Did the Buddha have to do homework?

The Buddha, when he was still Prince Siddhartha, had everything any kid of his era could ever want. But he did go to school and, yes, he had to do his homework. In fact, he is said to have learned 64 different languages and to have excelled at math and science. After Prince Siddhartha had studied for a few days with the wisest ministers in the kingdom, the teachers went to the king and reported, "Your Majesty, the Prince does not need us anymore. After only a few lessons, he has learned everything we have to teach him. In fact, he has taught us a few things that we ourselves never knew before!"

The Buddha wanted to do more than what was expected of him, so he made up his own program of study. The entire universe was his set of textbooks and the experience of life was his school.

Reducing pride

My older daughter is sometimes reluctant to tackle her homework or to take part in extracurricular events. She has described herself as "a stand-offish straight-A student who isn't like other girls." Pride has its good and bad points. On one hand, you need a certain amount of pride in the form of self-esteem. Positive self-esteem is feeling good about yourself, your appearance, and your accomplishments, but you can feel this sort of pride without *being* proud.

Being proud means believing you are special or better than everyone else. Pride keeps you from admitting that you are wrong—if something bad happens, it must be someone else's fault. Buddhists identify this sort of pride as one of the root delusions. It shows up when you are accused of some offense. The proud, haughty self, the "I, the Precious One," leaps up in outrage and denies doing anything. That outrage, that feeling that you are so great and so precious that you could not possibly do anything wrong, must be confronted and subdued.

In his book *Good Life, Good Death*, Gehlek Rimpoche describes an examination in which he was unable to answer some of the questions. He was on the verge of running away to become a "solitary meditator" when his teacher confronted him and reminded him that he was only learning, that he was a student and not yet a Buddha, and that he in fact had performed very well. Only a few mistakes made him want to run away (Rimpoche, 109). When he was told that making mistakes is part of learning, he decided to stay and continue his education with the other students. This choice turned out to hold many benefits for him and for his many students and admirers around the world today.

Tip: Incentives such as stars or points often motivate kids and give them a sense of accomplishment. Create a system of "accumulation of merit." The points can be redeemed for any reward you see fit.

DISCUSSION STARTER

I bet those Buddhist kids in Tibet don't have to work like we do

Learning, thinking, and understanding are essential components of Buddhism. The heart of the educational system focuses on the profound relationship between student and teacher. For thousands of years, Buddhist monks in Tibet, China, India, and other countries underwent rigorous education. In addition, the monks regularly debated to test their knowledge, and engaged in stringent oral examinations in which their knowledge was evaluated before other students and teachers. Tests weren't taken in private, by writing answers on paper, as they are done today.

In order to learn, you must read and comprehend. To convey what you know, you must have an understanding of grammar and the ability to write clearly. Each of these skills will help you progress spiritually as well as achieve good grades.

Today, Tibetan children go to school and study hard, if they are lucky enough to find a good school in which to enroll. Our family sponsors a young Tibetan woman who escaped the repression in her homeland and fled over the mountains to India, where she studies in a school for refugees. She regularly reports on how hard she is working. She cannot go home for the holidays to be with her family, but remains in the school to study.

DISCUSSION STARTER

This is so boring. Why do I have to do homework, anyway?

The Dalai Lama and many other Buddhist teachers for hundreds and hundreds of years before him had to go to extremely tough schools. They were tested constantly by debating points with other students. They had to memorize long prayers that didn't make much sense at first. But later on, the meaning became clear to them.

So don't rush through your assignments so you can just veg out in front of the TV. Find something that grabs you and think about it. For instance, maybe you learned in science class that it takes worker bees ten million trips between the hive and the flowers to gather enough nectar to make one pound of honey. Think hard about that one point for a minute. Ask yourself: "How does it make me feel? What do I want to do badly enough to make ten million trips to succeed?"

Take that single minute of thinking and carry it with you throughout the day as a memory of something cool that you learned in school. The next day, try to find two such minutes. The next day, try to find three.

If you have a bad day and nothing seems to go right, don't give up. Try again the next day to find one positive moment and start building up those tiny, positive moments once again. No matter what the subject, you can keep yourself from being bored. It all depends on making the cool stuff you learn part of who you are.

THINGS TO DO

Building motivation

If your kids are having a hard time doing homework or they're complaining about being bored in class, remind them that the fact is nobody can do what they like all the time. Sometimes you just *have* to do things. A task can be an unpleasant ordeal, something you just have to get through, or it can be a meaningful, uplifting experience. The difference is in your *motivation*—your reason for doing what you do.

Buddhists believe that the best reason for doing anything is because it will help other people. Tell yourself that your motivation for going to school, just for today, is to learn how to be a kinder and wiser person so that you can help others. Instead of comparing yourself to the kid sitting next to you, think about how lucky you are to be a human being who can learn and think. What lion in the jungle or aardvark in the zoo could possibly hope to learn such cool stuff? You might forget the capital cities of half the states as soon as the test is over, but the habit of using your brain will stay with you forever.

If your motivation for doing your assignments is to avoid being yelled at or to get a good grade, you'll have a tough time staying interested in your schoolwork. Instead, try some play-acting in your mind to build good motivation:

- Pretend that your homework assignment is a great gift that has been handed to you by royalty.
- Tell yourself that doing this assignment will help others through a terrible crisis.
- Remind yourself that you, and you alone, are fortunate enough to be able to do this one thing that will make the world a better place.
- Pretend that each problem that you do, each sentence that you write, and each fact that you memorize, is a single brick. Keep thinking that when you have enough bricks you can build a great monument to knowledge that will keep bad things from happening in the kingdom.
- When you are done with your homework, take a moment to picture in your mind that this single assignment has added to your own knowledge and the world's knowledge.
- Envision kids all around the world sitting at their desks after school and adding their bricks to the monument to knowledge.
- Each day, as more and more homework assignments are done, see the monument growing higher and higher like a great castle. Armies of ignorance try to attack, but the monument stands firm.

THINGS TO DO

Help your kids dedicate their efforts

After your kids have finished their homework, give them a coin to put in a jar. When the jar is full, help them give the money to a shelter for abused women or neglected children. This practice encourages children to consider not only how they benefit by finishing their homework—for instance, by being allowed to go outside and play or to watch TV—but also to think about others. It also reminds them that, even if their efforts don't seem to have any immediate rewards, they can one day benefit others.

Easing report-card anxiety

We live in a results-oriented society. We tend to judge ourselves, and we are judged in turn, by how successful we are—whether in a career, on a spiritual path, or at school. My daughters' anxiety about report cards and good grades begins long before the grades arrive. Despite my assurances that I'm proud of them whatever their grades are, they often say, with tightness in their young voices: "I hope my report card is OK."

If children could be induced to feel good about themselves regardless of their grades, report cards would lose much of their power. But when I talked with my 11-year-old on this subject, she asked me, suspiciously, "Do you know something about my report card? Did I get a bad grade?"

It became clear to me that all the preaching and meditating in the world won't relieve her anxiety altogether. The fact is, we *do* want our kids to get good grades, and those grades *do* count for something. You may not be able to eliminate your child's anxiety altogether, but there a few things you can do to help them put their feelings in perspective after the grades come in.

THINGS TO DO

Letting go of negative feelings about low grades

No matter what kind of evaluation a school system uses, the grades on the report card may not always reflect a child's level of competence. Perhaps your son reads books and magazines far above his grade level, but gets low grades in reading because he doesn't participate in class. Perhaps your daughter memorizes facts long enough to get an *A* on the test, but isn't able to apply what she has learned in other situations. Try these suggestions for reducing negative feelings about grades:

- Buy your youngster flowers, one for each grade. For instance, if your child gets three *A*s, a *B*, and a *C*, give him three carnations, one lily, and one rose. Help him arrange the flowers in a vase and let them enliven your home for a while. Remark on how all the beautiful flowers represent his good accomplishments. When the flowers have withered, rather than throwing them away, put them on a compost heap where they transform into material that will one day help new flowers to grow.

- Give your child practical opportunities to share what she has learned in each subject, quite apart from the grade on the report card. Ask her to read you a story while you're resting from a hard day, check to see that you got the right change when paying your bill in a restaurant, or explain the meaning of a difficult word to a younger sibling. Offer praise for how much she knows, whatever her level of understanding.
- Talk to your kids about the fact that even adults get "report cards" from their bosses or their customers.

Releasing unpleasant feelings about grades is like ridding yourself of the Eight Worldly Dharmas (fear of blame, desire for praise, fear of pain, desire for pleasure, fear of ill-repute, desire for fame, desire for gain, fear of loss). Encourage your children to visualize letting go of negative feelings as though they are black smoke leaving their bodies and being blown away on the wind.

How do you measure success? Spiritual and educational materialism

Buddhist teacher Chogyam Trungpa discourages practitioners against spiritual materialism—devoting time to practices that focus solely on tangible benefits such as experiencing visions, bending spoons, or achieving the ability to fly (Trungpa). Practices that emphasize inner development are a much better use of one's time and ultimately benefit a wider range of people.

There is nothing wrong with money and tangible results, of course. Money, comfortable homes, and good jobs give people the ability to take care of themselves and their loved ones. Good grades help students make the most of high school and are an asset in applying for college scholarships, but grades aren't the only measure of success. The ultimate measure is the one inside you. Ask your child:

- Did you do the best you could?
- Do you feel like you are learning and growing as school progresses?

If the answer to either of these questions is no, ask them:

- What can you do to feel better about school and how you are doing in class?
- Would you like to talk to your teacher about it?
- Should we talk to the teacher together?

Educational growth, like spiritual growth, occurs a little bit at a time. You may not notice a change when it occurs, but when you compare where you are today to where you were a year ago, you will see a difference. Encourage your children to think about how much they have learned in the past year and remind them that results are not always tangible.

Measuring success

If you're like me, you keep more samples of your child's schoolwork than you need. Now is the time to make use of some of those artifacts. Dig out some of your child's past schoolwork from different stages in their school career. Find a picture they drew or an object they made in preschool, then a project they completed in first or second grade, and so on. Place these samples on a table, in a line, and ask your child to look at them. Encourage her to see how much more capable she is than she was just a few years ago, and what a great leap she has made since she first entered school. Ask her if she sees evidence of her progress; tell her that this progress is still continuing, even if it doesn't seem to be as fast as she would like.

EXERCISE

Visualizing a positive outcome

My children feel most anxious when something is about to happen. The anticipation of visiting the dentist or greeting their friends at the birthday party causes the anxiety. After the experience passes, they inevitably conclude, "That wasn't so bad."

Buddhism has much to say about in-between states. Focusing on the positive and visualizing the outcome can influence what happens—or, at least, how you experience what happens. The ultimate in-between state is the *bardo*, the transitional state between birth and death. Tibetan Buddhists teach that the bardo is an opportunity to achieve enlightenment, and that by remaining positive during this critical period you can be reborn in a pure land.

One of my friends encourages her children to visualize a positive result whenever they feel anxious. It's a subtle way of conveying her Vajrayana Buddhist experience to her two sons. Vajrayana is a result-oriented practice in which you envision pure, ideal environments and see yourself as an enlightened being. My friend, of course, doesn't need to convey any of the esoteric and incredibly rich teachings of the Vajrayana to her children. She just teaches them to focus on a good outcome in all situations, and this is something you can do no matter what your spiritual tradition.

THINGS TO DO

Enthusiasm for schoolwork

Enthusiasm is one of my personal favorites among the Six Perfections, the six activities performed by Bodhisattvas (beings who are committed to helping others through love and compassion). The fact that enthusiasm as a spiritual activity generates tremendous positive karma as well as merit brings a new dimension to getting homework done or turning in reports. An assignment isn't just a task to get a grade or meet a requirement; performing the task diligently, on time, and with a positive sense of accomplishment is a sign of Bodhisattva activity.

Although it's important to meet standards set by the school, parents can add fun and enrichment by providing activities that make the school curriculum more meaningful. As you work on any of the following projects with your child, verbalize the good feelings of accomplishing your tasks.

- If your child is studying fractions, practice measuring or cutting wood using a simple pattern for an object such as a small wagon or footstool.
- If your child is studying biology, take a walk in the woods and identify plants and the footprints of animals.
- If your child is studying a historical time period or another country, research the clothes and food of that time or place. Prepare a representative meal together, dressing as appropriately as possible and including relevant objects as table decorations.

Praising your child with phrases such as, "I'm so proud of my little Bodhisattvas," or "That was a good way to be a Bodhisattva," will give a new dimension to homework assignments, no matter how mundane they may seem.

What would the Buddha do if he got a D?

If the Buddha got a *D*, he might have reminded himself that everything changes. Even a *D* doesn't last forever. It might turn into a *C* or *B* next time grades come out. He also might consider that, in a past life, he may have been an animal with no ability to study and learn at all. In comparison, being a human being with the ability to learn, think, meditate, and get a *D* seems pretty good!

EXERCISE

Let negative emotions come and go

Anxiety—like anger, jealousy, and other unpleasant emotions—is impermanent. In just a moment, something good can happen to turn your mood around: your best friend calls, you get an *A* on a test. Something happens that instantly transforms your agony into delight. Practice letting go of anxiety without being attached to it. Stand at the sink. Experience worry about burning your finger if you make the water too hot. Imagine your finger starting to burn, feel the stinging pain, and visualize putting it on ice. Now, turn on the cold water. Your anxiety vanishes. Ask your kids to try doing the same thing with their anxiety when they are waiting to get back a test or report-card results.

The five hindrances

Being anxious about passing a test or receiving a good report card, or doubting his ability to do well, can make your child feel bad. But the issue goes deeper than that. Along with the Five Precepts, the Four Noble Truths, and the Eightfold Path, Buddhism also identifies the Five Hindrances to spiritual progress:

- Doubt
- Lust
- Hatred
- Worry
- Laziness

As you can see, doubt and worry together make up 40 percent of the obstacles to spiritual progress. It's reasonable to assume that they can also be a hindrance to progress in school or other areas of life. The key to overcoming such hindrances is letting them go rather than becoming attached to them.

Dealing with bullying

When my daughter reports that kids in her class have been making fun of her, I first observe my own internal reaction. Anger and outrage rear their ugly heads within me: "How dare they do that to my daughter!" If I fail to rein in my thoughts, violent fantasies arise in which I storm through the school like some sort of parental Terminator, teaching respect by hurling threats like thunderbolts. But usually I am able to stop myself and listen to what she is saying without further distraction. The following phrases remind me of my responsibilities:

> *I can't solve my children's problems at school.*
> *I can't fight their battles for them.*
> *I can only give them the tools they can use to find their*
> *own solutions.*

You already have those tools at hand in the form of your Buddhist spirituality, though you may not be consciously aware of it. Offer them to your children with love and patience, and try to instill the same love and patience in them.

Fighting back doesn't necessarily mean fighting

The prevailing view in school is that those who are strong fight back when they are taunted, either with fists or with words. Teach your children that there are other ways to respond. The best way to show them is by your own example. If someone challenges you while you are out shopping or at a ballgame, respond the way you would want your children to respond—with patience and good humor.

A high-school student told me the following incident that involves a surprisingly old-fashioned rule, but that occurred just a few years ago:

> Buddhism helps when people are showing anger. One time I was at a football game at another high school, not my own high school. Someone came up to me and told me I was violating a fashion rule at this school and this was disrespecting them. When people get mad at you they might call you "stupid," and say things like "I don't like you; I think you're really mean." The impulse is to say, "I think you're meaner," and then it escalates. But I don't like to be in those situations.
>
> In this case I just said, "Well, can you tell me what's wrong?" The person said, "Well, you know you can't wear white after Labor Day in our school," and I said, "No, I had no way of knowing that," and that defused the situation. My friends said I was being a "wuss." But then I explained to them, "I can't be mad at them. You can see they are suffering too."

Such a realization can lead to compassion for other people, if your mind and heart are open to it. This is an exceptional young woman whose parents are both members of my Buddhist sangha. The difficult task that she has mastered is to realize that people who are bullying or behaving in a mean way are suffering, too. In the heat of the moment, as soon as name-calling or accusations are heard, it is difficult to turn the feeling of "I have been wronged" into "They are suffering, too."

THINGS TO DO

Turn words into flowers

Suggest that your son or daughter visualize a bully's words turning into flowers that cannot harm them. Gehlek Rimpoche has often told a story related to him by Ram Dass, the famous spiritual teacher. Ram Dass was at a family Passover gathering, and his brother-in-law was attacking and criticizing him. Ram Dass was able to visualize the words as arrows shooting toward his face, then falling harmlessly on the table. Encourage your children to visualize a scene like this taking place. Practice with non-threatening situations, such as a neighbor's dog barking incessantly, or a sibling practicing the same song over and over on the violin, and remind your child to "Visualize flowers."

DISCUSSION STARTER

What do you say when someone makes fun of you?

Try some role-playing. Your son or daughter comes to you and reports, "This kid is being mean to me all the time and calling me names."

"To win one hundred victories in one hundred battles is not the highest skill. To subdue the enemy without fighting is the highest skill."

Sun-Tzu, *The Art of War*

You say: "Why don't you talk to him?"

Your child says: "I don't know what to say."

You say: "You've got a choice. You can choose to respond in different ways. What you say will affect how the other person reacts."

Describe the possible responses shown below:

Your child says	Likely response
"You're an idiot, too."	"Oh yeah? Put up yer dukes and fight!"
"I feel really sorry for you."	"Nobody asked you what you think. Shut up!"
"I am sorry you feel that way, but I disagree." Then walk away.	Silence. No fight occurs.

Ask your son or daughter: "Which do you think is the most patient, compassionate way to respond?"

Standing up for yourself

Normally, you would not be physically rough with your daughter. But if she was in the road and a car was speeding toward her, you might grab her and throw her down to get her out of harm's way. Sometimes a physical response is called for, not only to protect yourself from harm but also to protect your attacker from doing something that will generate bad karma and possibly cause legal or disciplinary action. By fighting back when it's absolutely unavoidable, you might prevent the attacker from doing something worse at the same time that you protect yourself.

If someone comes at you with a weapon or prepared to throw a punch (and you're lucky enough to have a moment or two to consider the situation), you don't need to roll up into a ball and get hurt. Talking calmly may not stop the person from attacking you. The attack is already underway, so defend yourself.

The Buddha doesn't want us to be doormats. Yes, Buddhism is about nonviolence and about respecting others, even those who attack us, and exercising the pervasive patience that turns the darts of their words into flowers. But that is only one side of the

The mad elephant

There was once a king who tried to kill the Buddha. He decided to use a mad elephant—a creature used at that time in India as a weapon to kill enemy troops during wartime. Such an elephant had a special wheel attached to his tusk and this wheel would catch anyone who came near it. When the king heard that Buddha was coming to the area, he ordered the mad elephant to be sent out. Buddha's disciples all fled in terror from the animal, leaving Buddha alone. Buddha didn't run away, however. He simply remained calm and raised his hand. As he did so, the elephant saw not five fingers, but five lions. A Buddha's physical presence has extraordinary qualities. Similarly, your child's calm exterior can help to defuse anger.

story. Your children will have to stand up for themselves out of respect for themselves. Sometimes, they may have to fight back, whether with words, with a compassionate, patient attitude, or— if being physically attacked—with fists.

Gehlek Rimpoche tells the story about the time he was in Amsterdam, and he happened to be carrying a large sum of money. As fate would have it, he was heading down one of the city's narrow streets, when he noticed that someone was following him. The man confronted Rimpoche and attacked him physically, not only trying to get his money, but trying to hurt him. Rimpoche didn't have the time or leisure to provide a compassionate teaching to someone intent only on doing harm. He struggled with the thief, socked him in the nose, and ran off, money intact (Rimpoche).

EXERCISE

Try out different responses

Suggest to children that if they see someone else taunting or teasing another child they might try to get past the usual accusation of "You're wrong. You're a bully. That's terrible." Instead, encourage them to think of something different, for example: "How that person must be suffering, to cause such pain. Isn't it sad that the person is finding the only way to deal with the situation is to call names?" Ask your child: "What kind of response might you get if you said, 'I'm sorry you feel so bad about yourself that you have to make fun of people, but name-calling doesn't bother me'?"

Look into martial arts classes such as aikido, which teaches self-defense, and offer your children another path to spiritual development. These classes also develop self-esteem that can help children remain calm when someone tries to bully them.

The "Zen Master" and team sports

Sports and Buddhism go well together. Just ask Phil Jackson, coach of two world-championship professional basketball teams, the Los Angeles Lakers and the Chicago Bulls, and a former player himself. Known as the "Zen Master," Coach Jackson says the key to success in basketball is to "quiet the endless jabbering of thoughts so that your body can do instinctively what it's been trained to do without the mind getting in the way." If your kids are in despair because they just lost the big soccer match and they want to give up and walk away, encourage them to take a series of calming breaths. Ask them to visualize doing well. Build up their confidence. Remind them to focus on bettering their own best performance, not just on winning the game. If they use their ability to quiet their mind and concentrate calmly, they are likely to do better.

Competing in sports and other contests

In order to develop spiritually and emotionally, you also need to develop physically and take care of your body. Physical activities such as yoga, walking, and running can aid one's spiritual development. In fact, yoga, aikido, and walking meditation can each be considered a spiritual practice.

Unfortunately, most school gym teachers don't take the spiritual benefits of exercise into account when they provide an exercise program for their students. Gym classes often incorporate meaningless exercises or stress competition that some kids enjoy but that leave other kids feeling left out and rejected.

DISCUSSION STARTER

Would the Buddha ditch gym class?

Buddhism is about finding nonviolent solutions to conflict. Yet, many sports rely on forms of violence. Can Buddhists participate in sports and still be Buddhists? Of course they can. One of the Six Perfections, enthusiasm, teaches Buddhists to participate fully and diligently in dharma practice. But enthusiasm can be extended to worldly activities as well, along with the recommendation to apply one's body, speech, and mind in unity. This might mean becoming part of a team or achieving an athletic goal you set for yourself. It also might include visualizing a positive outcome. Attaining competence in these areas on the athletic field can be beneficial in many walks of life as well as contributing to good spiritual practice.

Are we there yet? Turning the wheel of "carma"

It's great if your children have plenty of chances to walk or ride their bikes from place to place, but chances are they also spend a lot of time in cars, buses, trains, or subways. A good part of a modern kid's day is also spent going from home to school, from school to after-school activities, from soccer practice to music lessons to doctor's appointments, and back home again.

Moving around can be neutral time—a time when you're not creating any karma, but simply focusing on the task at hand. But time spent in the car (or, as I like to call it, "carma") can be more than that. It can give you a chance to help your kids to become more mindful of what's going on around them.

 STORIES TO READ ALOUD

What kind of car did Buddha drive?

Legend has it that when Prince Siddhartha first ventured outside the walls of his palace to see the world, he was taken in a fine chariot, driven by a charioteer named Channa, and pulled by a horse named Kantaka. The same horse took the prince away from the palace for good when he began his spiritual journey. You might say Buddha drove a model 600 B.C.

Kantaka (one horsepower)! But the vehicle that the Buddha truly drove was his own mind. By calming his mind and learning to live fully in the present moment, he became truly happy.

The two main approaches to Buddhism are known as the "Lesser Vehicle" (Theravada Buddhism) and the "Great Vehicle" (Mahayana Buddhism). All Buddhists drive one of these two vehicles today. You might say, the Lesser Vehicle is a compact car, as it's designed to take only the driver to the place beyond suffering. If that's so, then the Greater Vehicle is a super stretch limo, as its purpose it to carry everyone to enlightenment.

THINGS TO DO

Driving meditation

What can you do when your kids are bored on a long car ride? Turn on a tape? Feed them junk food? Try silence for a few moments. Then encourage your kids to do the following:

- See how long you can sit in the car while simply observing what's happening outside your car window.
- Create your own video. Let your eyes be your camera. Point the camera out the window. Turn off the sound-track and focus only on what you're passing. Let your breath be your soundtrack.

- Think: "There goes a forest of trees; there is a field of corn; there is a neighborhood of houses."
- Your mind will inevitably wander. You'll wonder: "Who lives in those houses? What if I were a farmer and I had to plant and harvest all that corn?" Let go of those thoughts. Instead, focus on your breath and simply observe.
- See if you can do this for ten seconds. Then see if you can go for 30 seconds. Don't think about whether you like what you see or dislike what you see. Simply observe.

In an essay entitled "Driving Meditation," Kevin and Todd Berger suggest that driving is an optimal Zen practice, one that promotes both awareness and experience (Berger and Berger, 133). The authors suggest that you practice simply being aware of what is going on all around you as you drive. Try to keep your mind free of attachments and judgments. Notice how you are attracted to this billboard, that new car, the sign in the store window. Notice the judgments you make about how homes look or how pedestrians are dressed. Try to clear all that out and simply observe without qualification. See if you can do this for ten or 15 minutes a day.

Whether you practice driving meditation or not, your attitude behind the wheel is bound to have an impact on your children. One of my clearest childhood memories of my father is the way he drove—absolutely relaxed and serene, with one hand (often, one finger) on the wheel. It may not sound particularly safe, but he always seemed to be aware of where he was at every moment. If, like me, you have a tendency to express outrage at the irresponsible driving practices of those around you, try to use this opportunity to practice and improve. Speaking from experience, I can tell you that the habit of getting angry behind the wheel and expressing anger verbally will go away with persistent effort.

Shifting gears, shifting goals: a driving meditation

On the way to school (a 30-minute drive through city traffic), my daughters often ask me to sign tests or other school papers or provide money, and perhaps permission slips, for lunches, field trips, or school pageants. When we get to school, the children usually argue about who will get out of the car first. One daughter returns for her backpack. Other cars are waiting in traffic in front of the school. When I arrive back home, I realize I have forgotten to give my other daughter her dress shoes for the school concert. I drive back to school and am forced to wait for a long, long stoplight. When I deliver the shoes, my daughter's happy, grateful smile and hug make the whole morning's efforts worthwhile.

For several years, I used to perform these tasks in a constant state of irritation. I would yell, pound the wheel, express frustration at my daughters' behavior. I would arrive home exhausted and require a full hour to calm down and concentrate on my day's work. You are probably familiar with this sort of reaction. It is caused by the desire for everything to go smoothly, without any obstacles, and the belief that every obstacle is a burden keeping me from my ultimate goals: getting the girls to school on time and returning home to work.

Gradually, after long practice, those goals have shifted—or should I say evaporated. The need to get to school and get to work is still there, but it is no longer the ultimate goal. The process has become more important. Simply accepting that obstacles will occur, I watch them almost in amusement: "Ah, yes, there is someone right behind me, tailgating me, challenging me to be impatient. Ah yes, there is my daughter asking me to read her papers while I am driving. I am grateful for the time I have with my children. I do not have to put them on a bus. I do not have to commute to work. I am able to talk to them in the morning. Ah, how wonderful that is. Like the car, I can switch gears. I no longer go into fifth gear or overdrive. I stay in a lower, slower gear and watch it all go by me while I enjoy the chaos as much as I can."

Junior road rage

Driving, especially in urban areas, is full of constant challenges to one's patience. As the driver, you need to realize that your children are sitting right behind you, watching your example and soaking in every unkind word you mutter or every gesture you make in response to other drivers' behavior. Car time is a challenge for kids, too. When they are confined in a tightly enclosed space for long periods of time, they can easily become impatient and display their own form of "road rage" through arguments or even physical fights. Commuting by car or other vehicle can be a real-world opportunity for your kids to put spiritual beliefs into practice. By simply being more aware of what's going on around them while you drive, your kids can develop good habits that carry over into other parts of their lives.

Good karma and bad karma?

In order to fully appreciate "carma," you need to understand the basic concepts of karma. Karma is a system of cause and effect. You create your own karma, and your life experiences proceed according to your karma. To say that someone who ran into trouble had bad karma is to misunderstand the Buddhist concept of karma. It isn't a form of luck—good or bad. Rather, karma arises because of conditions, and those conditions arise because of your own actions. If you smoke and drink a lot, you create conditions that may eventually produce illness, for instance. If you study long and hard, you may gain knowledge and succeed in school. Karma has four characteristics:

1. Karma is definite but dependent on conditions.
2. Karma develops quickly, but can be stopped by purification.
3. You will experience a result, whether good or bad, if you created it.
4. You will not experience the result if you have not created it, no matter what you do.

If you clean and maintain your car properly, it will run smoothly until the body and parts wear out. If you drive too fast for conditions and veer into oncoming traffic, you will likely meet with a bad result. Just remember, you can always change your driving habits, take classes, and obey the speed limit and not have an accident, after all. Consciously choosing your actions will determine your karma.

DISCUSSION STARTER

Would the Buddha have whined, "Are we there yet?"

Because the Buddha never took a single trip outside of his palace until he was a young man, he probably didn't make a big fuss when he did go traveling. But when he was young and confined within the palace walls, he probably became antsy and anxious, as would anyone else. When you feel impatient, what happens? You expose yourself to the delusions of everyday life: to the suffering of wishing you were somewhere else, to the desire for some form of amusement, to the anger of being forced to wait, and to the ignorance of how fortunate you are to be able to go where you are going, instead of to the knowledge that everyone else in all the other cars has the same needs and desires—all of us just want to be happy, and not in such a hurry.

THINGS TO DO

Who made this car?

Next time your kids are bored or restless in the car, suggest that they think about all the things that went into creating the car itself.

- Ask questions that encourage them to consider that for thousands of years, people could only walk or use animals or boats for traveling.
- Ask them to consider who designed the car they are riding in and to guess how many different people played a part in putting it together.
- Ask them to name all the materials that went into making the car—steel, glass, plastic—and to realize that someone had to make each piece and mold it carefully to the correct size and shape.
- Talk about where these materials come from. For instance, glass is partly made of sand, and steel comes from iron mined from deep within the earth.
- Discuss how wonderful it is that thousands of cars are driven on the streets and how important it is for all the drivers to observe stoplights and traffic rules. If they did not, there would be chaos and undoubtedly many accidents.
- Remind your children that the only reason they can get from one place to another is because countless people all around the world did their own work and cooperated with one another.

- By the time your kids come to this conclusion, either they will have settled down or you'll have reached your destination.

Who's driving this vehicle?

Virtually all Buddhist sects fall into one of three schools, or vehicles. The word "vehicle" is derived from the Sanskrit *vada*, which means "ferry boat." The schools are all ferries that can take travelers across the river of life and deliver them to the opposite shore of enlightenment. Gehlek Rimpoche has had a good deal of fun with the word "vehicle" over the years. In his book *Good Life, Good Death*, he tells the story of a man in Hong Kong who asked, "You are telling me not to have attachment to nice things. What do I do with my Rolls Royce?"

Rimpoche told him, "As long as you are having the pleasure of driving the Rolls Royce, that is fine. But, if the Rolls Royce drives you, then you are in trouble." (Rimpoche, 96)

This wisdom applies to automobiles as well as horses, oxen, or spiritual development. In other words, don't let yourself be carried away by emotion. Stay on course and stay focused. Keep your eyes on the road. Anger, attachment, and other delusions are like wild horses, Rimpoche teaches. When you see a wild horse coming toward you, let it go by. Similarly, when someone runs a stop sign or cuts you off in traffic, you have a great chance to practice letting go. Let the delusion of anger pass you by and stay focused. This will set a good example for your children when they get behind the wheel themselves, or when they're passengers in someone else's car.

The three vehicles

The two most prevalent schools are Theravada and Mahayana. Mahayana is known as the "Great Vehicle" because it emphasizes enlightenment for all beings, while Theravada Buddhism or "Lesser Vehicle" emphasizes education and a monastic life that leads one to become an arthat—someone who has achieved freedom from suffering. The third, Vajrayana, is also called Tantric Buddhism. It might be called the "Turbo-Charged" vehicle because a Tantric practitioner has the capacity to attain enlightenment extremely quickly—even within one's current life.

PART THREE

Teaching values and beliefs

Some children seem quite certain about their beliefs. Oprah Winfrey interviewed a group of schoolchildren in Chicago, asking what they understood about what happens after death. The Christian children explained that you go to either heaven or hell. In heaven you received candy; in hell you were burned. But when the child of one of my sangha members was asked who God was, she simply said, "I don't know." When she was asked what happened after death, she said, "I don't know." It was a traumatic experience for her to respond with honesty and admit her uncertainty.

This doesn't mean you need to indoctrinate your children with absolute certainty that the Buddhist cosmology is the one and only truth or that they ought to memorize everything about the hell realms and pure lands. As Rabbi Steven Rosman points out, there's a difference between religion and spirituality:

> *First and foremost, spirituality refers to an intense, personal, awe-based concern for questions about life and meaning, as opposed to religion, a traditional collection of institutionalized and canonized doctrines, rituals, rites, and creeds about those same questions. I believe that religion is born out of spiritual experience.*
> (Rosman, 6)

Buddhists are able to separate their spirituality from their religion to a greater extent than most faiths. You can meditate and practice generosity and patience without ever reading the Buddha's words directly. But many inquisitive children want to know, "What do Buddhists believe? If I decided to become a Buddhist like my parents, what would I believe?" Parents who are unsure of the answers themselves may have difficulty answering their questions. We often know what to do without having a firm grasp on why we do it. Timing is important: when children express curiosity or when they are open to teaching, that is the time when your words will have the most impact. The questions that naturally arise when a pet or a relative dies can serve as teachable moments that give you the chance to convey your Buddhist values and beliefs. At such moments your words aren't just empty preaching—they become spiritual exercises that enable your children to learn about your experiences. You will have the chance to awaken your children to the beauty and majesty of life, to help them realize how precious life is, to evoke wonder, to strengthen their self-esteem, and to develop their compassion for other beings.

Teaching your children about the Buddha

Children are naturally curious about the Buddha's life. They are surprised to learn that, unlike Jesus, he was born into great wealth and privilege. He gave up power and luxury the moment he became aware of the suffering in the world. Why would he give up all the good things in life—not to mention his home, his wife, and his family—to live the life of a monk? The specter of old age and death brought about the dramatic change.

The story of the Buddha contains the element of adventure. Buddha wandered the countryside seeking a teacher and trying to find a way to transcend the cycles of birth, rebirth, and suffering that are collectively called *samsara*. He battled the evil spirit,

Mara, and finally achieved enlightenment under the Bodhi Tree. He then devoted the rest of his life to sharing teachings that changed the world.

What can children learn from the story of the Buddha? They learn that he began his life as an ordinary being who transformed himself through his own efforts. His life was the opposite of a rags-to-riches story: rather than defeating other people and working hard to achieve wealth, he began life with everything anyone could ever want and ended up a relatively poor monk. On the other hand, he discovered that living as an ascetic was going too far, so he found a middle way, a balance, to achieve his goal. He used his curiosity, his insight, and his persistence to learn the ultimate truth about life.

Tell the story of the Buddha when your children wonder why they have to work so hard in school, or what purpose book learning and reasoning serve. When they protest against an experience they think is useless, such as a particular sport, camping in the woods, or sitting quietly by oneself on a sunny afternoon, explain to them that all experiences have value. The Buddha achieved an enlightened state after experiencing virtually everything life had to offer and then finding his own path.

DISCUSSION STARTER

Why is the Buddha so fat?

The way the Buddha is physically depicted differs from country to country. Most images show the Buddha in a serene, contemplative pose. That's the historical Buddha known as Buddha Shakyamuni. The Buddha to come in the future, Maitreya, is often depicted as fat, jolly, and laughing. The Buddha's physical characteristics demonstrate his spiritual accomplishments:

- The *ushnisha*, or round bump, atop the Buddha's head symbolizes his enlightened mind.
- He has a mark in the center of his forehead representing the Wisdom Eye.
- He has long, hanging earlobes.

The historical Buddha and other Buddhas who have appeared throughout history are each said to have 29 marks that designate them as enlightened beings. A Buddha's physical appearance is said to be welcoming so that students will be attracted to him and want to learn from him.

STORIES TO READ ALOUD

The Buddha's life, part I: The Buddha was a kid like you

Note to Parents: Consider adding your own reminiscences about when and where your children were born when you read this part to them. If any of your stories involve a bris, a christening, or a baptism, this would be a good time to weave them in with the Buddha's story.

The Buddha's real name was Siddhartha Gautama, and he was born around 566 B.C. to a royal family living on the border of northern India and southern Nepal. He was born in the spring of the year, around the time when the moon was becoming full. Siddhartha's father was King Suddhodhana, and his mother was named Queen Maya. Like any parents, they dreamed about what their son might grow up to be one day. His parents were so happy to have an heir to the throne of the kingdom of Shakya that they gave him the name Siddhartha, which means "every wish fulfilled."

A group of Brahmins were invited to a feast at the palace shortly after Siddhartha was born, so they could tell the baby's future. They predicted that he would either become a powerful king or a wise religious leader. They warned that if he ever left the palace, he would pursue a spiritual life. But if he could remain within the walls of the palace, he would eventually become king. King Suddhodhana wanted his son to be ruler of the land, so he decided to keep his son cloistered within the walls of the palace. He surrounded his son with beautiful things and luxuries in the hope that he would never want to leave. Siddhartha was a good student; after they had taught him for a while, his teachers would have to tell the king that he had learned everything they had to teach. Rather than horsing around with his young playmates, he kept to himself, spending time with the wild animals that lived in the palace gardens.

Once, a flock of swans flew overhead. All at once, an arrow shot through the air, and one of the swans fell to the ground. The arrow had gone right through its wing. Siddhartha went to the swan and gently picked it up. "You poor swan," he said. "Let me help you." He pulled out the arrow and took off his own shirt, wrapping it around the wound. After a while, Siddhartha's cousin Devadatta came up. He was carrying a bow and some arrows. "Siddhartha, I shot a swan! Help me look for it!" Then Devadatta saw his own arrow on the ground and the swan resting in Siddhartha's arms. "Hey, that's my swan!" he cried, grabbing at the bird. But the prince protected it and refused to give it up. Siddhartha suggested they go to a court of adults, who would decide what to do. The two appeared before the king and his ministers. The boys described what had happened. The ministers themselves ended up arguing about what to do.

Finally, an old man came into court. The boys repeated their story, after which the old man declared, "Everyone loves his or her life more than anything in the world. Therefore, the swan should belong to the one who tried to save its life, not the one who tried to take its life away. Give the swan to Siddhartha." So it was decided Siddhartha would keep the swan. But when the king tried to find the old man to thank him, he had mysteriously disappeared. Everyone thought that Siddhartha must be a very exceptional prince that such events would occur in his life.

"The teachings of the Buddha are like a recipe for fresh-baked bread. Thousands of years ago someone discovered how to bake bread, and because the recipe was passed down for years and years, you can still make fresh bread that you can eat right now."

Pema Chodron, "Not Preferring Samsara or Nirvana".

STORIES TO READ ALOUD

Buddha bedtime stories

The Jataka Tales are a series of stories told by the Buddha himself. They describe his own adventures in previous lives, when he appeared in many forms and at many times and places to relieve the suffering of all beings. I highly recommend the series of books adapted from the Jataka Tales and published by Dharma Publishing. *The Hunter and the Quail* tells the story of a group of birds that works together to escape a hunter's net; it teaches children the value of cooperation. *The Rabbit Who Overcame Fear* shows how knowledge can help beings overcome their fear. These books are richly illustrated and include drawings that kids can color.

Sharing Buddhist practice with your kids

One of my fellow sangha members told me that on her daughter's seventh birthday, the child asked her how to meditate. My friend began to explain how to sit quietly and visualize light and loving feelings going out to all beings, bright as sunshine. "Well, I do that already!" her daughter exclaimed, and skipped happily away.

Have an open-door policy when you do your practice. This lets your children know that you are available for them. On the flip side, it also reminds them that, although you are meditating, they don't have free license to raid the freezer, throw their toys around, start a food fight, or run outside without closing the door. Expect this open-door policy to provide you with some challenges. Your children, if they are young, may come in and cuddle with you or sit with you. They are just as likely to jump on the cushions, touch the candles, and yank statues off the altar. My own teacher tells about students who can sit on their cushion generating love and compassion but, the moment someone bumps their cushion or bothers them in some way, they become enraged, snapping at people to leave them alone. "Can't you see I'm generating love and compassion?" Think about what kind of message this sends to your kids. Instead, sit still and let them be near you as long as they don't spill water or set the room on fire. Remember, they have come to teach you. You have summoned these enlightened beings to help you with your spiritual development. Don't chase them away when they arrive.

A man once told Thich Nhat Hanh that he had been practicing for ten years but his daughter did not know what he was doing. Thich Nhat Hanh admonished, "If you practice correctly, then your daughter should know what you are doing and she would be able to participate. Otherwise, your practice will not bring happiness and peace" (Eastoak, 98).

Art projects and activities

You can use art and craft projects to communicate Buddhist beliefs and values to your children. Here are a few suggestions:

- Hold a scavenger hunt to let your child find and gather all the parts of an object. When assembled, the object might be a puzzle, a model, or a house, for example. Help your child with assembly. When the object is complete, experience taking apart the design as a way of demonstrating impermanence. In this way, the object is similar to the intricate spiritual drawings called mandalas that Buddhist monks spend many days creating with sand only to scatter the grains upon completion.

- If you have a computer with Internet access and a Web browser that can run the Java applets found on many Web pages, look for sites that allow kids to create their own mandala-like designs online.

- Create a totem pole. Most children are familiar with totem poles as made by First Nations people. Affix Buddhist motifs to various-sized boxes and stack them to make your own version. You can also use clay to create a totem or a diorama in a shoebox.

- Put on a play. At family or neighborhood gatherings, my girls and their friends love to direct and act in plays. Come up with Buddhist themes for skits (the *Jataka Tales* are good sources) or prepare a puppet show.

- Connect the dots. Make your own dot-to-dot pictures or puzzles depicting the Buddha or other spiritual images. It's fun to draw scenes on pieces of paper, tape them together, and create a scroll using two cardboard tubes.

Provide incentives for positive actions

Spiritual development can be condensed into a single, simple statement: reduce your negativity and transform negative thoughts, words, and deeds into positive actions. Or, as the old song "Ac-cent-tchu-ate the Positive" by Johnny Mercer and Harold Arlen prescribed:

You've got to accentuate the positive, Eliminate the

negative, Latch on to the affirmative, Don't mess with
Mr. In-between.

You've got to spread joy up to the maximum, Bring gloom
down to the minimum, Have faith, or pandemonium's
Liable to walk upon the scene.

Buddhist brain teasers

Brain teasers are a big hit, whether you're sitting around the dinner table or stuck in a traffic jam on the way to the piano lesson. Kids in primary grades get a kick out of one-word-wrong sentences. Get them started with some examples, and then encourage them to make up their own. Here are a few statements pertaining to Buddhism that you can use not only as brain teasers, but also for mini-reviews:

1. John imagined love and good wishes spreading out to all robots in the universe. [substitute "beings" for "robots"]
2. Jane imagined that her anxiety and nervousness were washing away as she washed her enormous trunk. [substitute "hands" for "enormous trunk"]
3. On Thanksgiving, Brad went from door to door, giving water balloons to the poor. [substitute "food" for "water balloons"]
4. Elizabeth felt great peace and openness as she arranged pots and raked harmonicas in her garden. [substitute "plants" for "pots" and "leaves" for "harmonicas"]

It sounds simple, but all practitioners know how difficult it is to break old habits of worry, impatience, criticism, and anger. One of the best things you can teach your children is to start good habits early. Teachers and parents have used incentive systems for generations. In the classroom, students are still given stars when they complete an assignment; parents still give rewards for doing chores around the house. It's a practical example of how karma works: do something good and, eventually, something good will happen to you.

Using a reinforcement chart is a great way to translate a value into something concrete and tangible. Rather than money, which emphasizes material rewards, try to think of reward systems that are likely to change a young person's negativity into positivism. You might offer a shared experience in exchange for a certain number of points earned. My daughters are particularly fond of making a cake, playing a game of checkers, or going to a zoo or museum.

Bringing meditation into the home

Breathing is a gateway to the soul, and an effective way to change our state of mind. When you are angry or nervous, your breathing becomes shallow and short, and your chest becomes tight. Think about when your children were babies. Did they breathe that way? Of course not. Their breaths were long, deep, and relaxed. Sometimes, when you watch children sleep, it seems as if they are not breathing at all because their breaths are so effortless and complete. If you and your children can recapture the ability to breathe fully, you'll become more relaxed and better able to cope with emotional distress. You can then learn to use breathing as a meditational tool. By focusing solely on the breath, you can calm the mind and learn to be mindful.

Creating a breathing space

Vietnamese monk and Nobel Prize winner Thich Nhat Hanh suggests that families set up a breathing room—a room where they practice only breathing and smiling, especially during difficult moments. When a conflict arises, before you or your kids get angry, ask them to go to the breathing room rather than allowing the fight to escalate. When they are ready, they can ring a bell to invite others into the room or, when they have calmed down, they can come out and try to resolve the conflict in a calm and loving manner.

The space you create should be different from other parts of the house. Consider creating a rule that anyone who enters the space must remove his shoes or don a special garment, in order to set the space apart. The scent of incense will also help create a peaceful atmosphere.

Create a call to prayer

How many times have you seen your child sit down to do homework only to stare at her blank sheet of paper with a dreamy look in her eyes? How many times have you had every intention of meditating but instead started to compose a shopping list in your mind? Sometimes it helps to have a visual or audible signal.

Many traditions use a bell as a call to prayer. You can ring your own bell or another device; the Tibetan finger cymbals called *ting-sha* make a high, clear, and easily heard sound. Incense also helps to create a calming atmosphere that encourages everyone in the family to be quiet, contemplative, and focused on the task at hand. Your signal can be as simple as a hand-drawn image pasted on a small wooden stick held up by a lump of clay. When your signal is in place, you are telling the world that you mean business about focusing on your assigned task.

THINGS TO DO

Practice breathing

Silence is a precious gift that you can give your children. If you are able to teach your children the benefits of mindful meditation—or just the ability to watch their own breath for a minute or two at a time—you will have given them a tool they can use for the rest of their lives. For now, start small. Encourage them to get in the habit of breathing— breathe in, breathe out, in the pattern of this mantra taught by Thich Nhat Hanh:

In, out
Deep, slow
Calm, ease
Smile, release
Present moment
Wonderful moment

Just as breathing can influence your state of mind and moods, so it also can affect your children. Kids who are unhappy or distressed will benefit from learning to take ten deep breaths, slowly and deeply. The time to teach this is not when they are upset, however, but at a time when they are calm and receptive. You can share the following meditation with your children and encourage them to relax. When they are in need of calming, they will have this experience to call upon:

1. Sit quietly, either on a cushion or in a chair, with your hands on your knees or in your lap. Consciously relax your body and quiet your mind.
2. Imagine that it is summer and the sun is creating a wonderful warmth. You are on a beach, sitting in a comfortable chair, and the waves are rushing in to the shore and then receding, one by one.
3. Close your eyes and feel the warmth of the sun on your hands, on your feet, and on your face.
4. Take a long, deep breath, beginning with your diaphragm, which is located in your midsection, above your stomach. Expand your stomach as you breathe—try to make your breath come from deep within rather than from up around your lungs.

5. Keeping your stomach expanded, continue inhaling from your lower chest, your lungs, and finally your throat. Imagine that peace and well-being in the form of bright light is filling your body.

6. Hold your breath for a count of ten, if you can—if not, count as high as you can and then exhale slowly. As you exhale, visualize that all of your negativity is leaving your body in the form of dark smoke. The dark smoke leaves through your hands, through your feet. Try to exhale slowly, so that your stomach is fully retracted.

7. Inhale again and take a long, deep breath, continuing to feel the warmth of the sun and hearing the peaceful sound of the waves rushing on the shore. Imagine that the cool water comes up around your feet. Hear the sound of the waves turning into foam as they sink into the sand and tickle your toes. Continue to breathe in and out, feeling your body being filled with warmth and health and peace and positive energy as you inhale. As you exhale, feel all negative feelings are leaving you just like the waves that sink back into the sea.

8. Take ten more deep breaths in this way. When you are done, sit quietly and enjoy how you feel. Carry the relaxed, warm, positive feeling with you as you return to your everyday activities.

As you can tell, this is a good meditation not just for kids but for everyone else in your household, too.

Mindfulness meditation

The term "mindful" can be defined in several ways. The most common, everyday meaning is being aware of your actions and their effects. Another way to define mindfulness—one that is observed by many Buddhists—is the act of watching the mind. That's all: just being aware of what your mind is doing at any particular moment.

Explain to your children that the mind can jump from one thought or emotion to the next with great ease and tremendous speed, like a monkey leaping from limb to limb. It's easy for your mind to run away and carry you along with it. One moment, you are happy; the next, you are plunged into the depths of despair. Why? It's all thanks to your monkey mind and its habit of reacting to situations in unenlightened, even harmful, ways.

In the *Sattipatthana Sutta*, also called the Sutra of Mindfulness, the Buddha emphasized to his disciples the importance of breathing as a way of learning to be ever mindful:

> *Mindful, he breathes in, and mindful, he breathes out. He, thinking, "I breathe in long," he understands when he is breathing in long; or thinking, "I breathe out long," he understands when he is breathing out long; or thinking, "I breathe in short," he understands when he is breathing in short; or thinking, "I breathe out short," he understands when he is breathing out short.*

> *"Experiencing the whole body, I shall breathe in," thinking thus, he trains himself. "Experiencing the whole body, I shall breathe out," thinking thus, he trains himself. "Calming the activity of the body, I shall breathe in," thinking thus, he trains himself. "Calming the activity of*

*the body, I shall breathe out," thinking thus, he trains
himself. (Thera)*

While attempting to follow the mind as you breathe in and out,
see where your mind tries to wander—you may feel strange
doing this; you will hear distractions in the house or sounds outside; you remember something you read or saw on television.
Each time your mind wanders, bring your attention back to your
breath.

STORIES TO READ ALOUD

The Buddha's life, part II: The Buddha's search

*Note to Parents: There are many ways to make your
mark on the world, and many choices you can make.
You might share some anecdotes about your own choices
on your way to becoming a parent, as well as your own
spiritual quest, as you tell the story of the Buddha's
youth and spiritual search.*

Prince Siddhartha learned to excel at a warrior's activities, such as swordsmanship and archery. He eventually married a young woman named Yasodhara and
together they had a son. One day, Siddhartha heard
someone describe the beauty of a spring in the forest
outside the castle. Siddhartha begged his father to let
him go outside the palace walls for the first time.

127

The king realized that he couldn't keep Siddhartha within the palace forever. But he could control what his son would see when he got outside. So he ordered all the old, sick people to go into hiding. So it was that, when Siddhartha came outside, driven by his charioteer Channa and pulled along by his favorite horse, Kantaka, everywhere he saw only healthy, happy people.

But as it happened, four signs appeared to him on four separate visits outside the palace. First, Siddhartha saw an old man with white hair and wrinkled skin wandering by, leaning on a staff. Siddhartha asked his servant, Channa, what he had seen. Channa explained that this was an old man, and that everyone would grow old one day. Siddhartha was shocked. On his next trip outside the palace walls he saw a man who was coughing and moaning and grabbing his stomach. On the next trip, he spotted a funeral procession along with a corpse. In this way, Siddhartha discovered sickness, old age, and death, and realized that there was much suffering in life. On his final trip, he saw a man with a shaven head, dressed in robes. He seemed peaceful and serene. "Who is that?" Siddhartha asked.

"He is a spiritual seeker, someone who tries to solve the mystery of sickness, old age, and death," replied Channa.

"Ah, that's what I want to do," said Buddha.

And that is what happened. When Siddhartha returned to the palace where everyone was singing and dancing happily, he knew that this was not the kind of life most people led. He resolved to search for a way out of the suffering that everyone eventually experiences. He left the palace and took to the country to begin his quest.

When bad things happen

Unpleasant occurrences are part of the suffering of life. Chicago Cubs fans know this all too well. Living near Wrigley Field, I tell my children about the *dukkha* (suffering) of baseball. If you are a die-hard fan of a soccer team that never seems to win the big game or if you follow a golfer who always comes up short in pursuit of the major championship, you learn to experience the present moment and hold no expectations. The moment you begin to expect a particular outcome, such as the division championship or making the World Series, you will be let down. As a Cubs fan, I practice my own form of Zen on a regular basis.

Purify your mistakes

One of the most valuable lessons I have learned from Buddhism is the fact that any non-virtuous action can be purified. Purification, in the traditional Buddhist sense, means that you can erase the imprint of the negative karma you receive as a result of a negative act. When you die and your negative and positive karma is tallied up, any negative karma that you have previously purified won't count against you. If your children can grasp this concept, so much the better. But even if they cannot, they can still relieve feelings of guilt and help undo the impact of their mistakes by purifying them. A well-defined set of steps exists for purifying mistakes you have made or actions that (whether intentionally or unintentionally) end up hurting someone else. First, the traditional version:

1. **Recognize who has been harmed.** For offenses such as stealing or lying, other human beings may be harmed. Buddhism teaches that the enlightened beings are harmed when we break our vows or make other spiritual mistakes.
2. **Take an antidote action.** Saying the Refuge Prayer and generating a sincere feeling of love and compassion for all beings is one way to purify the negativity.
3. **Generate regret.** You feel bad about what you did—but not so bad that you get caught up in guilt. You dislike what you did and you realize that it was not good.
4. **Promise not to repeat the action.** A promise not to repeat follows naturally upon regret. You resolve that you will not repeat the non-virtuous action.

These four opponent powers of purification can be simplified for children. You have probably seen a child who has broken something cower in fear, crying, because he is afraid to confess the mistake. The child is preoccupied with the fear of punishment. This fear tends to block out the fundamental realization: "I have done something wrong." Instead of taking responsibility, the child is thinking: "I'm going to get it now." The child's focus is inward, on what's going to happen to him, rather than thinking of the consequences of his actions for other people. By reacting patiently and with love, you can defuse the situation and enable the child to look outward. You can explain: "You did something wrong. Now you feel bad about it, but there are steps you can take to make things better. Let's run through the four of them together."

1. **Acknowledge what you did.** Say out loud, calmly and without crying, "I [your child should describe the offense]. I hurt/harmed [your child should describe who was hurt or who suffers as a result]."
2. **Apologize.** Say you are sorry for what you did, and take action to lessen or undo the damage—get a bandage for your friend; clean up the mess; tape or glue the broken object.
3. **Realize that you did something that hurt someone else.**
4. **Promise to try not to do it again.**

Simply recognizing that the relevance of a negative action is the suffering it causes someone else is a profound realization for a young person and the start of a positive habit. Praise your child and remind her not to dwell on what happened or continue to feel bad about it. Then, apply your own advice to yourself. Not long ago, when my daughter broke an antique pencil during a temper tantrum, I calmly worked through the process with her, but I found that, while she felt better, *I* had some residual feelings of loss and anger. I *did* like the pencil and was attached to it, after all! I rejoiced that the breaking of the pencil had given me a chance to practice patience and help my daughter work through her fear of being punished. I also rejoiced that she responded in a positive way. I meditated for a moment on the impermanence of all things, including pencils. This lessened my feelings of attachment and loss considerably—though I'd still like to find a replacement for that pencil to put back in my collection some day.

Showing respect for life

Think about the practical, visible ways in which you can convey your spiritual values to your children. You can meditate with them, say a prayer before meals, and celebrate significant days of the year. From asking young people what practices have had an impact on their thoughts and behavior, I have learned that the Buddhist respect for the lives of all other creatures, especially flies and other household pests, is one of the most influential.

If you find a fly or spider in your house, try to catch it and release it outside instead of killing it. This may be difficult, and it may not always work, but it is just the kind of thing that impresses kids. It conveys the essential lesson that the lives of all beings, no matter how small and seemingly insignificant, are important.

At first, you may not think that running after a spider with a plastic container and carefully taking it outside will have any impact. Your children may even ask with some bewilderment exactly what you are doing. This is a signal that they are open to a little teaching. Explain that it's important to respect all creatures, no matter what they are, and that you have made a commitment not to harm or kill anything if you can help it. Don't worry if they shake their heads or roll their eyes at first. It takes a while for this concept to sink in.

When I asked the teenage daughters of my fellow sangha members what their parents had taught them that encouraged them to become Buddhists themselves, they immediately referred to the fact that their parents had always refused to kill spiders and other pests. Your own commitment to nonviolence and your personal example of compassion has a tremendous impact on your children.

What's wrong with killing a spider?

Killing a spider encountered in the house may be such a casual act and such a long-term habit that it seems natural. Taking the time to trap the spider in a container and carry it outside to free it may seem unnatural because it is so unusual. What's wrong with simply doing away with a spider, or with other pests in your home, such as ants or cockroaches?

While it may be tempting to make a speech about the non-virtuous karma of killing or overtly connecting this act to Buddhism, you don't have to do so; the gesture speaks for itself.

Q. How can we keep from killing bugs without knowing it, when we're driving or walking?

Q. Why should we care about a spider or bug in our house? What's wrong with just squashing it?

Sometimes, you can't help killing household pests. If it's a choice between having fruit flies land in your juice or letting mice run around freely versus doing away with them, you may need to consider the health and safety of your children first. As a compromise, I purchase the mousetraps that consist of plastic squares with sticky glue designed to catch the mouse alive. On a couple of occasions, my daughter and I have taken the mouse out to a field and laboriously peeled the animal from the trap with the flat side of a knife. We were able to free it still alive, though it did have lots of glue on its body. We avoided the karma of killing, though I can't say we avoided the karma of causing the mouse to suffer. But we just can't have mice running around the house, and I did purify the suffering I caused, so it's a compromise I can live with.

Caring for pets

One of your ultimate goals as a Buddhist parent is to convey a sense of respect and care for other beings. It's difficult to do this with creatures that have no close connection with children and that may be not be cute and cuddly, such as flies or moths. It's much easier and more practical to instill a sense of love and compassion in children by encouraging them to care for a creature they already enjoy, such as a pet.

Give your children the responsibility of caring for another living being. Discuss it with them first and impress upon them the responsibility of maintaining an animal's health and well-being. Buy them a pet, such as a fish, bird, or cat. Consider getting a pet of your own as well; you might even get one pet for each member of the household. Children will notice how you treat your own pet—it's a good way to convey a gentle sense of caring.

At first, your child will be keen to take care of their pet. After a while, this enthusiasm naturally fades. While they are still happily cleaning cages, draw up a schedule by which they will feed and clean up after their pet on an ongoing basis. You may have to remind them of this, but your job will be made easier if you have both agreed to a contract beforehand. You need only point out the contract to remind them of their responsibilities.

Accepting change

Change is an inescapable part of being a parent. Every time you turn around, it seems, your son or daughter has grown into someone different. The more you love them, the more you want them to stay the way they are at any particular moment; you don't want them to grow older. As novelist Neil Gordon pointed out in an article called "The Pity of Love," love and loss are part of the everyday experience of all parents: "To love children deeply is not only to risk a catastrophic loss; to love children is also to lose them over and over again, on a daily and momentary basis, not as they die, or move away, but as they, simply, grow (Gordon, 69)." But it doesn't stop there. Just as you are learning to deal with the fact that you are losing your children even as they grow—or even if you are only able to acknowledge that such change exists and are unable to accept it, you are still required to teach your children how to deal with change in their own lives. Rather than tackling big changes, such as moving to a new town or new school or coping with divorce, start with natural changes like the seasonal transitions.

THINGS TO DO

A summer journal and fall scrapbook

Making scrapbooks is a growth industry in some communities, but how many have a spiritual theme? Take photos of your spiritual community's leader and

other folks you see on a regular basis. If you go on
retreat, preserve a leaf or a bird feather from one of
your walking meditations. Print out e-mails and save
programs or invitations of meetings and celebrations.
And, of course, save plenty of space for your child's
own poems and drawings. Creating scrapbooks
together as a project is part of the fun, but don't forget to enjoy your collections when you have some
free time or hear that familiar cry, "I'm bored."

Have your child make a drawing or painting of
something nice that happened over the summer. This
is a perfect activity for the last days of summer, just
before school begins. Then gather photos and turn
them into a collage. My daughters and I arranged and
framed about twenty photos taken during the summer of 1999—a visit to an amusement park, picking
cherries in the backyard, a birthday party, and so on.
Now we have a visual record that we can refer to all
the time; even years later, it makes us feel warm just
to look at it.

The Four Noble Truths for kids

The Buddha's teaching on the Four Noble Truths conveys a rich
understanding of human life and all the change, impermanence,
and emotional highs and lows that go along with it. The traditional teaching communicates four fundamental insights:

1. There is suffering in life
2. The suffering you encounter has a cause
3. You can end your suffering by ending the causes
4. There is a path that can bring freedom from suffering

This "path" is sometimes described as the Eightfold Noble Path consisting of: Right View, Right Intention, Right Speech, Right Action, Right Livelihood, Right Effort, Right Mindfulness, and Right Concentration. For children, the Four Noble Truths are sometimes simplified and then encapsulated by the acronym "BIIG." BIIG stands for four basic truths about life that are taught in virtually all schools of Buddhism:

1. Life is a Bumpy Road
2. Life is Impermanent
3. Life is Interdependent
4. Life can be Great (Nirvana)

You don't need to teach this out of context. Wait until there is a bump in the road and mention it in the moment so that it will have relevance to your son or daughter. You can then expand on the BIIG version of the Four Noble Truths as follows:

Life is a bumpy road

Young people can better relate to this choice of words than to "Life is suffering." The word "suffering" is charged with stigma. The misconception that everything in life is just suffering or that life equals suffering is not what the Buddha taught. Simply recognizing that bad things as well as good things are a part of everyday life is helpful. Suffering is natural and therefore many people experience it.

Life is impermanent

One of the biggest reasons is that nothing is permanent. All living beings die, and whatever state something is in now will change. If we are comfortably warm one moment, we may be too warm the next. One aspect of the fundamental facts of change and impermanence is that we are never satisfied with what we have. We want something more, or we want something to be different.

Suppose your child does something unacceptable and you take away television privileges for the evening. Your child, not surprisingly, responds by pouting and refusing to speak to you. Rather than remonstrating or arguing, let the youngster stew in his own juices for a few minutes. Patiently say: "I understand that you are angry, and I know why you are angry. It's impermanent. It will go away. Things will get better." Don't say anything else. Let ten minutes go by. See if the anger fades and your child becomes willing to talk again. In this instance, you can be thankful that everything is impermanent.

Life is interdependent

We often don't recognize that we are all equal and dependent on one another for our happiness and survival. Instead, we focus on the differences in the way we look, the way we dress or speak, and the way we act. In fact, we are all the same, and we all need one another. Everyone started life as a baby with the same basic needs, and everyone wants to be happy. Think about the stoplights and speed limit signs you see as you drive from one place to another. Every individual driver or passenger is dependent on the other drivers around them. The passenger is dependent on the driver observing the law and not making foolish decisions. The driver depends on other drivers to stop at stop signs and red lights. If people didn't obey these laws, accidents would happen everywhere, yet many people drive as though nothing can happen to them or anyone else. This fundamental misconception causes many of the speed bumps and potholes that we encounter on the road of life.

Life can be great (Nirvana)

Simply realizing that things can get better *for you*, that *your* life can be great, is a new realization for many children (not to mention adults). The italics are added for emphasis because modern culture provides no shortage of reminders of how *some* people's lives can get better. You may not realize it can happen to *you*, and you can make *your* own life better by changing the way you view people and events. Instead, you see news reports on people who won a fortune in the lottery, movie stars that make millions, celebrities who can afford mansions and sports cars. There's nothing wrong with money. But it isn't what makes you truly happy, deep down inside. And you can't take it with you when you die. Your life can be great if you accept that things are impermanent, that all people are the same and dependent on one another, and if you learn to let go of the bad things that happen to you and focus on good things as well.

STORIES TO READ ALOUD

The Buddha's life, part III: What the Buddha found

Note to Parents: As you read this last part of the story, mention the steps you have taken on your own spiritual path, something that occurred to you on a retreat, or a

*beautiful place where you once meditated. Tell them
about what you learned along the way.*

Siddhartha wandered the countryside for several
years, trying to understand why there was so much
suffering in life for so many. His desire for understanding was fueled by the people he saw around
him. He saw a man working hard, plowing a field
with the help of two big oxen. As the plow turned
over the earth, many little bugs and insects were
turned up. Some were killed; others scattered in con-
fusion. Birds that had been singing happily a moment
before swooped down to eat them. The oxen were
working hard; the farmer was sweating as he whipped
them to keep them moving.

"This man works so hard all day just to feed his
family. They just want to be happy. But look at all the
misery and pain that results. It seems so awful." The
prince's heart was filled with compassion for all of
these beings—the insects and birds and oxen, as well
as the farmer. He sat down quietly under a rose apple
tree and thought about it. Just sitting quietly he
became calm, and experienced (for the first time) a
wonderful stillness. His mind was clearer than ever
before because his thoughts were quiet. "Everyone
just wants to be happy," he thought. "Instead, everyone has to work so hard, and they get sick, they grow
old, and they die. All the pleasures of the world that I
have had just come and go. I, too, will get sick and
grow old and die. There must be a way to end all this
suffering."

Siddhartha went from one teacher to another, trying to find the way to relieve the suffering he saw all around him. For six years, he tried all kinds of different things. He grew his hair long and put it in a ponytail; he cut his hair very short so he was almost bald. He tried yoga. He tried starving himself, thinking that by controlling how much food he ate, he could also control himself and his senses. He became so thin that his bones showed through his skin. Finally, he thought, "I'm not getting anywhere. I haven't learned anything. It's a mistake to punish myself like this. All the pleasure I had doesn't work, and all this pain doesn't work. There must be a middle path—a path between pleasure and pain." He remembered when he sat beneath the rose apple tree and felt so peaceful and calm. "Maybe I should try to meditate like that again." But he was so thin and weak he could hardly move.

It happened that a young girl named Sujata lived nearby in a village at the edge of the forest. She had just given birth to her first child and she was very happy. She took some food into the forest so she could offer it in thanks to the spirits she believed lived there. When she encountered Siddhartha sitting there, thin and weak, she offered the bowl to him. He ate gratefully and felt much better. Siddhartha began to meditate under a tree that is now known as the Bodhi Tree. He said, "I will not get up until I have reached my goal." He sat under the tree for a whole day: 24 hours. During the night, an evil spirit named Mara tempted him with thoughts of food, beautiful

music, dancing, and all the things he had left behind.
Then Mara sent his armies after the prince.

Siddhartha's mind was filled with thoughts of pain
and terrible things—he imagined the armies shooting
him with arrows and clubbing him. Still he sat quietly. Then the evil Mara filled Siddhartha with doubt:
"You're no good. You can't do anything. Who do you
think you are, anyway?" Siddhartha had a hard time
sitting still and thinking these thoughts. He reached
down and touched the earth, asking for clarity.

Finally, he had a series of great realizations. He realized that suffering is infinite and is an inescapable
part of birth, life, and death. He also realized that
there is a way out of suffering—that we can escape
the cycle ourselves by meditating and changing our
own minds and habits, by being kind to others, by
avoiding harm to others, and by being as positive as
we can. Siddhartha had awakened to the great knowledge, and that is why he is called the Awakened One,
the Buddha.

Explaining reincarnation to your kids

Don't expect your kids to fully accept or understand the concept
of reincarnation all at once. Have faith that they do understand
when it comes to spiritual practice, even when it seems nothing
is sinking in. One of the times they may be more receptive to this
concept is at the death of a pet, a family member, or a friend.

Telling my daughter that her pet hamster may have experienced a better rebirth thanks to all the happiness he provided and all the love he generated in her seemed to help soften what seemed like an immense tragedy.

THINGS TO DO

Buddha in the bud: gardening as spiritual exercise

The lotus plays an important role in Buddhism. It grows from a seed with a very hard shell that looks like nothing living could ever come out of it. For the lotus to grow, you must first make a little hole in the shell so that water can come in. Bury the seed in mud and make sure it gets a steady supply of water. Before too long a plant begins to sprout. Eventually, the plant grows out of the mud into something incredibly beautiful. In the same way, you can grow spiritually through the shell of your ego by making a little hole in it. (The ego is the set of assumptions by which you define yourself.) Once spirituality takes root, you can grow like the lotus, right through the hard shell and mud, and emerge as a new and beautiful person, one who is generous, patient, and kind, and who is dedicated to nonviolence and to helping other beings.

Plant a lotus seed and watch it grow, or plant a vegetable garden in the spring. Discuss what spring means in terms of physical rebirth and liken this to spiritual rebirth. You might also discuss your own childhood religious experiences and explain how you discovered Buddhism and what it means to you.

Helping your children deal with death

As I write this, my daughter is in mourning for a pet hamster that died. I have discovered that, despite my efforts to save the animal and my desire to minimize my child's pain, there is nothing I can do to protect her from her disappointment. I can't change her feelings, but I can ask her how she is feeling or suggest that she write a poem or draw a picture of her pet. I can even help her stage a funeral. These are some of the ways that I can be present for her as she deals with death.

DISCUSSION STARTER

What happens after we die?

This is a profound and complex subject and, as you may know, Buddhism offers a tremendous amount of information designed to help people achieve a "good death," one that propels them toward a good rebirth. Just how much information can children absorb about this concept? They are probably already aware of the idea of heaven as being a "better place" after death. What they may not know is that how they live affects how they die, and the amount of love and positive karma that a being generates has a bearing on one's rebirth. Build on what your kids already know without contradicting it. Explain that there are many possible places where a being can end up after death. They may experience a human rebirth, which will give them the capacity to improve their lives and the lives of others. Praying for a good rebirth might help a dead person on his or her way after death.

THINGS TO DO

Having a funeral for a pet

When a pet dies, stay with it for a short time to help ease its passage. Think positive thoughts and pray for a good rebirth. Tell your children that the care and love lavished on the animal surely created good karma that will help it find a better rebirth. It's possible the pet came into your son or daughter's life in order to provide just this teaching—how to love and care for a creature and provide it with the happiness and positive energy that would help it find a good rebirth. A funeral, complete with a headstone bearing a drawing or the photo of the pet, can help children externalize their feelings of sadness and prepare them to let go and move on.

Do Buddhists believe in heaven and hell?

As a Buddhist parent, you have a rich set of teachings you can call on when asked this question by your children, or should the occasion arise for other reasons. Since the Buddhist conception of hell is far more detailed than the Christian concept of a single fiery place, you can first describe the hell realms, the terrible places where people with bad karma go after death. Your kids will be fascinated by hearing about the eight hot hells, the eight cold hells, the nearby hells—and how a soul can arrive at any one of them. As far as heaven goes, you can discuss the pure lands, the paradises where Buddhists hope to go after death. One of these is known as Tushita, the land where the Buddha Maitreya—the Buddha of the future—lives now. The Wheel of Life, which depicts the various realms of existence including the hell realms, provides a vivid visual "map" that will intrigue your children.

Appreciate your time together

I often ask my children about their favorite parts of our days together. I also try to make a conscious effort to be balanced and, although my first impulse might be to sweep a disappointment or a scuffle under the rug, I try to help them inventory the sad as well as the happy. Perhaps the best part of a given day was one in which we solved a problem or overcame a difficulty.

Allen Ginsberg's death

Allen Ginsberg, the famous poet, was a dedicated and advanced Buddhist practitioner. He studied for many years with Chogyam Trungpa Rimpoche and later with Gehlek Rimpoche. I was fortunate enough to meet him several times and studied with him in the years leading up to his extraordinary death in 1996. Ginsberg's death is a teaching in itself. When he was told that he had incurable liver cancer, he surprised himself at how well he took the news. He immediately began finalizing his affairs and calling all of his friends and acquaintances. He also began writing an enormous volume of poetry. His death in his New York apartment was as open as his life. Between 80 and 100 people were present. In one area of the apartment, a party was going on. In another, Buddhist prayers were being offered. He invited those present to take souvenirs. He stopped breathing at 2:38 a.m. on the morning of April 5, 1997, but according to observers his consciousness remained in his lifeless body until nearly 11:30 the following night.

PART FOUR

Holidays

When most Westerners hear the phrase "happy holidays," they think of Christmas or Hanukkah, followed by New Year's Eve and New Year's Day. Other widely observed holidays—such as memorial days, independence and Thanksgiving holidays, and national celebrations have turned into more of a cultural routine than a time to remember the past or celebrate spiritual renewal. There's no escaping the candy, toys, billboards, advertisements, and store displays that summon citizens to follow the same display of consumerism as everyone else: you take the day off to eat and watch a parade or exchange gifts.

For parents, holidays can easily become just another exhausting routine, a source of extra work as you pack, drive, unpack, cook, eat, wrap, unwrap, and otherwise "celebrate." You may feel the need to take a day or two just to recover from having so much fun. Kids are more likely to adore holidays, not only for the enjoyment that comes with time off school, but also for the opportunity to see relatives they don't regularly visit, to go to new places, or to receive gifts.

The problem is that on such occasions nothing changes for you or your kids on the *inside*. Many parents who have been celebrating the same holidays in the same manner with their children year after year wish they were more meaningful—that these days were less about candy and toys, and more about love and compassion. In fact, each of the traditional holidays has deep significance that is frequently overlooked. The meaning can be brought out in your prayers and meditations.

Questions naturally arise. How does Buddhism fit in with the holidays that are usually celebrated in Western culture? Can you integrate Buddhist beliefs with Christmas, Easter, and other mainstream Christian holidays? Can you add some Buddhist festivals to your calendar?

As Thich Nhat Hanh says: "If you want to build American Buddhism, you have all the ingredients, all the elements, within your own culture, within yourself, your family structure, and your religious institutions" (Eastoak, 98). In other words, we should start with the traditions we have already and blend in what we have learned from the Buddhist teachings. Of course the same is true of all Western cultures where Buddhism is practiced.

Parents who follow the Buddhist path don't have to stop celebrating Christmas or Hanukkah. It is important that all generations continue to respect the traditions that their families still celebrate. Buddhist parents can enrich the seasonal holidays by being more mindful about the true meaning of those days. They can also add new meaning by celebrating Buddhist seasonal observances, many of them joyous events that are popular in other countries but little-known in Western cultures.

This part examines some ways in which you can better integrate Buddhist beliefs and Western holidays. It is possible through concentration, visualization, and detached self-reflection to put commercial influences in perspective and continue to grow and develop mindfulness.

Buddhism all year round

On certain days of the year, many Zen Buddhist temples are festooned with lanterns and prayer flags. Once a year, on Buddha's birthday, the monks and lay members of the temple parade through the streets, waving flags, carrying images of the Buddha, and ringing bells. The neighborhood kids may look on with great curiosity and wonder what's going on.

Kids love holidays and feast days, no matter what tradition they celebrate. In many countries around the world, Buddhist families celebrate significant days. In contrast to the Western schedule of holidays, the Buddhist series of important dates is remarkably informal. Some cultures celebrate Bodhi Day, the day on which the Buddha attained enlightenment, on December 8. Others celebrate it on December 25. The Buddha's birthday is observed in May in some cultures, in June in others.

THINGS TO DO

Develop your own celebrations

For Western Buddhists, the message is clear: choose the holidays you want to observe and when you want to observe them. Adding some significant Buddhist feast days to your calendar will enrich your celebrations and help balance Western with Eastern traditions. When working to instill a value, it's helpful to be specific and work on one at a time. You can also use a large calendar to designate a week or two as Patience Week, Tidiness Time, or Helpfulness Month.

Celebrate Bodhi Day—December 8

Bodhi Day, which many Buddhist sects observe on December 8, comes at the perfect time for those who are committed to Buddhist ideals of compassion and generosity. The day that marks Siddhartha Gautama's enlightenment comes just when you are beginning to scurry around and open your pocketbook. It is an especially appropriate time for you and your children to think about other people and explore your Buddhist practice. One Buddhist parent suggests hanging a decoration with three ornaments on your door to symbolize the three jewels of Buddhism: Buddha, Dharma, and Sangha. If you can encourage your children to create such an ornament and attach it to the door themselves, you will have provided a spiritual activity.

Here are some more ideas I gleaned from the Family Dharma Connections website. The website address is *http://www. pulelehuadesign.com/familydharma*.

- Along with (or instead of) the usual pine, spruce, or fir tree for Christmas, buy a ficus tree for your home. Why a ficus? The Buddha sat under the Bo tree (*Ficus religiosa*) when he attained enlightenment. You may not be able to find *Ficus religiosa*, but a more common *Ficus benjamina* will serve as a good substitute. Decorate the tree with lights and other beads on December 8 and keep it decorated throughout the holidays.

- There are many different ways to achieve enlightenment. Hanging multicolored lights of the sort commonly used at holidays literally "enlightens" your home and serves as a reminder of the different paths to enlightenment. You can turn on the lights on the evening of Bodhi Day and each night throughout the holidays. (You can also light a candle each night beginning on December 8 to represent enlightenment.)

- If you have a heart-shaped cookie cutter, you can make holiday cookies that are the same shape as the leaves of the Bo tree.

A Pittsburgh newspaper reported that a local Zen Buddhist temple celebrated Bodhi Day with a traditional meal of pumpkin, *kombu* or dried seaweed, shiitake mushrooms, garnish, tofu, and burdock. Zen practitioners brought out traditional lacquered bowls known as *oryoki*. They used the bowls during the seven days of *sesshin*—a silent retreat leading up to the Day of Enlightenment.

Give Hanukkah a Buddhist twist

There's no reason why Buddhists can't give gifts, visit with their families, sing carols, eat special foods, and enjoy all the other activities that are associated with Christmas and Hanukkah. You can do all of these things and still give the holidays added meaning by creating some new traditions.

For instance, the eight nights of Hanukkah can be nights when you symbolically burn off each of the eight worldly dharmas or eight worldly concerns. When you place candles in a menorah, create eight little paper boats as well. Label each one with a variation of one of the eight non-virtues that your children will understand:

- Desire for people to say nice things about you
- Fear of being blamed
- Desire to be famous
- Fear of people saying bad things about you
- Desire for a lot of money
- Fear of not having any money
- Fear of getting hurt or becoming ill
- Desire to feel good

Each night, when you light a candle, burn up one of the paper boats. Let the ashes accumulate in a coffee can or large bowl. On the last night, mix up all the ashes to show your kids that all of the worldly dharmas are the same. Go outside and scatter the ashes to the wind to symbolize letting go of the dharmas.

Observe Winter Solstice—December 21

Some Buddhists who don't normally celebrate Christmas or Hanukkah celebrate the Winter Solstice Festival instead. They bring a small, live tree into the house to decorate and plant it after the holidays. If you are unable to do this, you can take your cut tree to a park district site to have it turned into mulch. In return, you may receive a little sprig of tree that you can plant later. On Solstice Eve, the parents turn off all the lights to symbolize the shortest day of the year and the time when plants die. Then the children turn the lights on, one by one. They might meditate on a loss experienced in the year just past. Then there is a procession of children carrying candles or lights, proclaiming the return of the sun. The evening may conclude with a feast and gift exchange.

Give Christmas a Buddhist twist

While conducting daily meditation with your kids, explain that Christ was an enlightened being who sacrificed his life for others in the ultimate act of generosity. When you collect and wrap presents to put under the Christmas tree, set one present aside for all sentient beings. Make this a delectable food gift such as cookies or candy. When you are opening your brightly wrapped boxes, share this gift with all of those present.

In addition to bringing a Buddhist flavor to the holidays, your Buddhist practice provides you with a routine. Every day is a day to rejoice and worship, not just December 25. The end-of-the-year holiday time, when normal schedules are overturned, can be disorienting. Having a daily practice to turn to can provide you with a stabilizing force and help you cope, especially when traveling or entertaining. The stress of family gatherings can test anyone's patience and equanimity. Turn to your practice daily—in fact, make all of your shopping, eating, and connecting with family a part of your practice.

Observe Losar—late February/ early March

The celebration of the Buddhist New Year, called *Losar* in Tibet and India and *Songkran* in Thailand, occurs in different times of the year in different parts of the world. Cambodian and Laotian children enjoy a playful New Year's tradition in which they have a talcum powder and shaving cream fight. Why not stage such a "celebration" yourself?

The Tibetan observance of Losar (*lo* means "year" and *sar* means "new" in Tibetan) occurs on the first day of the first month of the lunar calendar. New Year's Eve, the 29th day of the 12th month, is a day of cleaning and preparation for purging yourself and your home of the accumulated negativities of the previous year. Traditionally, a special noodle soup called *guthuk*, or "ninth soup," is made. The soup contains nine ingredients and everyone is expected to eat nine bowls. The dumplings in the soup contain objects that indicate the person's personality: salt in the dumpling is a good sign; chili indicates a person who speaks roughly; coal indicates someone who has a "dark heart"; a white stone represents a long life; butter indicates that someone is sweet. Some families slip messages written on pieces of paper into the dumplings in the style of fortune cookies.

The guthuk soup is easy to create with a packaged mix for soup with dumplings; your kids can help form the dumplings and add objects or notes to them. You then mix them up in the soup and everyone will receive a special fortune.

Follow the moon

The moon is of preeminent importance in the Buddhist calendar. Every month, four important days occur based on the phases of the moon. Many of the important Buddhist holidays occur on specific days of the lunar calendar, and those days vary from year to year. Get a lunar calendar for the current year, or even consider obtaining a telescope so you and your children can get more in touch with the moon as a harbinger of feast days and auspicious days for engaging in spiritual practice.

DISCUSSION STARTER

Don't put all your eggs in one basket

Easter is a perfect time to discuss death and rebirth, but you can also use this opportunity to discuss balancing needs and desires. There's nothing wrong with traditional Easter egg hunts on Easter, but this year gently ask some questions to give your kids some things to think about.

Q. What is greed? What is too much, what is enough, and how does it feel to always want more?

Q. What would happen if you only gathered a certain number of eggs and then stopped and said, "That's enough."

Q. Why does that seem strange? Why do we always want more?

Encourage them to practice restraint; for example, don't consume all the eggs all at once, but try to space them out over several days (if not more).

STORIES TO READ ALOUD

The prince and the elephant

The Jataka Tales comprise a collection of 550 stories recounting the previous incarnations of the Buddha. Together, the tales illustrate the perfection of virtues on the path to enlightenment. The following tale can be connected with Easter and Christ's ultimate sacrifice. In this story, the Buddha is born as Prince Vessantara, a man renowned for his generosity. It's best to read this story in its entirety, and you can find a complete version at *http://seasiancrafts.com/spiritworld/jataka.htm*. The following is a brief summary:

On the day of the Buddha's birth, an auspicious white elephant was also born and was given to the newborn as a childhood companion. Years later, a delegation of Brahmins arrived from a neighboring kingdom and explained that their citizens were suffering from famine and drought. They beseeched the eminently generous prince to donate his white elephant because they thought it would help relieve their suffering. Prince Vessantara gladly granted this wish, then poured water over his guests' hands to signify that he did not expect them to repay him. Vessantara performed many acts of ever-greater generosity over his lifetime. He eventually relinquished even his own children. His generosity met its strongest test when a god descended and asked Vessantara for his wife as a servant. When Vessantara agreed to this request, the gods bestowed blessings upon the prince and he was finally reunited with his wife and children.

Observe Vesak—Buddha's birthday

The Buddha's birthday is variously called Wesak, Vesak, Visaka, or Visahka Puja. Buddhists celebrate the birth, death, and enlightenment of the Buddha on this one day. The date falls on the first full moon in May and is considered an important day for purification. In many Buddhist temples and centers, there is a tradition of bathing the Buddha. Practitioners wash the statue of the Buddha with great reverence and care. You can easily perform this same ritual at home. The Buddha's birthday can also be a day for cleaning the altar and all the offerings on it. Take the bowls down (be sure to pour the water into plants rather than down the drain) and help your kids wash the altar and the statue of the

Buddha. In May, flowers should be easy to find, so assign the younger children the task of gathering some fresh flowers from your garden or yard to place on the altar when you put everything back together. Emphasize that you are not only cleaning the offerings and the statue, but also clearing away your anger, attachment, ignorance, pride, and other negative emotions.

Why not give your children a small gift for Buddha's birthday? Fly prayer flags, or consider flying a kite to which you have tied prayer flags, as a way of celebrating. Since the Buddha was our teacher, children can use Vesak to express gratitude for those who teach them. Encourage your children to do something nice for their own teacher on this day: bake them some cookies or give them a card and the proverbial apple.

Remember the poor on Kathina Day— October

Kathina Day, which occurs on a full moon day in the 11th lunar month (usually in late October), is a robe-offering ceremony, in which the laypeople gather to make formal offerings of robe cloth and other items to the Sangha. Historically, townspeople gave the gift of cloth, and the entire community took part in the process of sewing the new robe before dawn of the next day. This ritual is still observed in some forest monasteries in Burma and Thailand. When offering the robes, the participants often say, "May we, venerable sirs, present these robes together with the other requisites to the Sangha. So, venerable sirs, please accept these robes and the other requisites from us, for our long-lasting welfare and happiness."

This is a great occasion to teach your children generosity. If you don't know any Buddhist monks, you can give warm clothing to the homeless or poor and wish them well. You might also collect canned foods and donate them to a food repository. Teach your children to say, "We give these clothes or food to help every needy person in the world."

Observe the Festival of Floating Bowls—November

Loy Krathong, the Festival of Floating Bowls, occurs on the full moon night of the 12th lunar month (usually November). People bring bowls made of leaves and filled with flowers, candles and incense sticks, and set them afloat in the water. As the bowls float away, all bad luck is said to disappear with them. The traditional practice of Loy Krathong was meant to pay homage to the holy footprint of the Buddha on the beach of the Namada River in India. If you want to get rid of negative feelings or experiences, this is a terrific way to do it.

Glossary

Bodhisattva: A person who has achieved enlightenment or is capable of achieving enlightenment but is putting it off in order to save all other living creatures. Bodhisattavas have love and compassion for all beings and use the skillful means informed by wisdom to help those beings attain enlightenment.

Buddha: A man by the name of Siddhartha Gautama who lived in India 2,500 years ago and who began the Buddhist religion. The term is sometimes used to refer to someone who has attained enlightenment ("a Buddha" or "a living Buddha").

Dharma: In an ultimate sense, this term refers to the teachings of the Buddha. In an immediate, temporal sense, it refers to one's own spiritual development.

Eight Non-Virtues/Eight Worldly Dharmas: Eight activities that keep one trapped in samsara. These eight activities are: fear of blame, desire for praise, fear of pain, desire for pleasure, fear of ill-repute, desire for fame, fear of loss, desire for gain.

Four Opponent Powers of Purification: Four activities that can be followed in order to purify a negative action: acknowledgment of who was harmed by the action; recognition that a negative action was performed and that it hurt someone else; regret for the action, often shown by an apology; and a promise not to repeat the action.

Karma: A complex system of cause and effect. It states that you will meet with the consequences of your actions unless you undo those actions. Positive actions will bring positive results, and negative actions will bring negative results.

Nirvana: The state of peace achieved when one escapes samsara through the realization of ultimate wisdom.

Pure Lands, Hell Realms: Regions where a being can go after death, depending on the sum total of one's karma. A great deal of positive karma accumulated through prayer and positive action can lead to rebirth in a paradise known as a pure land. Negative karma can lead to rebirth in one of six hell realms, some hot, some cold, some in which beings experience great hunger, some in which beings experience terrible pain.

Reincarnation: The belief that after death one is reborn into a new life, the nature of which is determined by the positive and negative karma accumulated during one's previous life.

Samsara: The cycle of recurrent suffering desire, repulsion, happiness, and despair repeated in life after life.

Sangha: Traditionally, the term refers to a community of monks. In modern times, it has come to mean the group of people with whom you meditate and learn—a Buddhist spiritual community.

Six Perfections: Activities that a Bodhisattva tries to achieve: Generosity, Patience, Morality, Enthusiasm, Concentration, and Wisdom.

Three Jewels: Buddha, Dharma, and Sangha are the basic components of Buddhist belief.

Appendix: Ten steps to mindful parenting

Step 1: Lay the foundation

The first step toward mindful parenting is to care for yourself and your own spiritual and emotional development. In order to be kind and compassionate to your children, you have to be kind and compassionate to yourself. In order to teach your children to be mindful, you need to be aware and mindful yourself. Make an effort, every day, to be a living model for the dharma. Children, like adults, learn more quickly if they have an example to follow. Think of the spiritual models you follow yourself. Buddhists all over the world follow the examples of various gurus. Think of the example set by the Dalai Lama: a selfless man who describes himself as "a simple monk" and who is continually smiling.

Begin with your motivation. Take stock. What prompted your interest in Buddhism? What does being a Buddhist mean to you? You have chosen to be a parent, not a monk. Parenting is about being fully immersed in life, not retreating from life. Rejoice in this decision and realize that you will be challenged. You may not be a monk, but you should retreat sometimes—whether it's for an hour, a day, or an entire week to help yourself recharge your batteries and soothe your soul.

A retreat might be as short as a walk around the block or a cup of tea in the garden. Being compassionate might mean doing something for yourself, such as seeing a movie *you* want to see, hiring a babysitter for the evening, or taking a few minutes to meditate or do your daily practice.

Step 2: Let your children teach you

It's easy to attempt to control the household by raising your voice and exerting your authority. It's more difficult to be open to what your children have to teach you. Your children will push your buttons. Not only that, but they will challenge you exactly where you need to be challenged. Realize that, as a parent, you will feel more anger, more impatience, and more exasperation—and experience more downfalls—than you would otherwise. It won't immediately seem like you are fortunate when you lose your temper with your children. But you are fortunate. Be happy that your children are there and that you are helping each other learn and grow together.

Children will, in fact, teach you their own version of the Four Noble Truths:

- Children break down your self-centered, self-cherishing ego, which produces suffering.
- Caring for children shows you how beings are interdependent and intertwined, which cuts through ignorance, the cause of suffering.
- Selfless love for children can end suffering.
- The goal of being a good parent and raising children well can dramatically further your own spiritual path and development.

Practice letting things go the moment your child drops and breaks a cup, calls to you to break up one of their disputes, or says something that irritates you. Realize that children learn by suffering and that your attempts to control everything can lead them to negative experiences.

Step 3: Develop moment-to-moment awareness

The fatigue of parenting, financial worries, and health problems can distract you from your children. Before you know it, they are no longer children. Your worries have dwindled, but your children are no longer there. Is bringing up children a chore or a celebration? While they are with you, learn to drink in the electricity of each moment with your kids. Listen to the wisdom of each moment. As Sandy Eastoak says: "A calm and spacious mind allows for a compassionate heart. After the children go to sleep, I take time to concentrate on unfinished household tasks; slowing down and focusing in a quiet environment clears tension" (Eastoak, 261).

The way you approach daily chores can make a dramatic difference in your outlook. My usual habit is to sigh and struggle through the dishes, the sweeping, and the picking up, as though they were all burdens placed on my exhausted body. When I make an effort to be mindful as I work, the load lightens at once. My heart and mind grow happier. This mindfulness includes an awareness of why I am doing these tasks and an appreciation of how fortunate I am to have young children to clean up after. Take the time to appreciate each article of cute, colorful clothing as you sort it—your kids will outgrow it before too long. When you clean up after dinner, rejoice that you were able to put food on the table and that you had the time and ability to serve it to these precious beings who are in your care.

Practice mindful dishwashing, mindful laundry folding, and mindful sweeping and straightening up. When you are done, take a moment to dedicate your efforts and rejoice over what you did—even if it was half-completed or imperfectly done. Focus on what you did accomplish rather than what you didn't do. Over time, your mood and attitude will grow more positive as this mindfulness becomes a habit.

Step 4: Practice visualizing a positive outcome

If you see your children fighting, throwing things, complaining about being bored, or having too much homework, be an island of stability for them. Solve the problem in your own mind. Visualize how the problem would be resolved if only you could take on their suffering and make them happy. Such meditation gets you out of your usual obsession with yourself and your own intensely personal dilemma. If your child is worried about an upcoming test, encourage her to visualize it turning out all right. If she responds, "That's just superstition. How can that work?" just ask her to try it and see what happens. If one of your children is in distress or fighting with a sibling or a playmate, practice exchanging their bad feelings with your good ones. Take on their trouble and imagine it being exchanged for boundless love.

Step 5: Pick the right time

Only convey little tidbits about your spiritual beliefs when the kids are ready to listen. It doesn't do any good to tell them to exercise patience when they are pouting in their room after a fight and don't want to hear you. Tell them after a few minutes when they have calmed down and are tired of being alone.

Remind yourself of spiritual stories and values so you will be ready when an opportunity arises. "I have a question" is a statement that indicates a receptive child. Redirect the conversation toward what you are trying to convey. If your child finds a bird nest, has a scary dream, or skins her knee, seize the teachable moment to be used for your purposes.

Step 6: Be accepting and tolerant

In order for kids to know how to behave, they have to know how to misbehave. His Holiness the Dalai Lama, who is without question a well-behaved person now, has written about fights he had with his brother and other ways in which he misbehaved as a child. Consider this excerpt from the "Parent's Tao Te Ching" by William Martin:

> If you want your children to be generous,
> you must first allow them to be selfish.
> If you want them to be disciplined,
> you must first allow them to be spontaneous.
> If you want them to be hard-working,
> you must first allow them to be lazy.
> This is a subtle distinction,
> and hard to explain to those who criticize you.
> A quality cannot be fully learned
> without understanding its opposite.

Step 7: Don't stop your own spiritual progress

Use your efforts to convey your spiritual values to your children as a means to enhance your own understanding and appreciation for your practice. Often, you don't study until you have to teach someone else or lead a discussion group. You may get so wrapped up in your children's lives that you don't attend as many teachings or keep up with your spiritual group the way you used to. This is natural, but keep reading and learning and meditating as much as you can.

The concept that "It takes a village to raise a child" applies to Buddhism as well. Don't assume that childless people in your study group will be put off by your children. Quite to the contrary, it can be a win–win situation as your child enriches their lives and they enhance the life of your child. Form an official or unofficial childcare co-op with other Buddhist parents. It's great to have your children reconnect with friends, for example, at an annual Buddhist retreat.

Step 8: Practice non-attachment

Non-attachment means "letting go." It often seems that raising children is a continual process of learning to let go of them for longer and longer periods of time. Practice with overnight sleepovers, then sending them to summer camp. Sending your child to camp is a big step. Every day that your son or daughter is gone, meditate on how you are working to overcome attachment and rejoice in your own progress—even if you are having a hard time and it seems as though your progress is minimal.

Instead of "snoopervising" your children, let them work out differences with playmates or siblings on their own. Instead of portraying yourself as the ultimate authority for solving every problem or answering every question, let them go to other adults for mentoring. Instead of feeling alienation of affection when your children bond with other adults, know that their interest is an extension of your own love and care. Realize that seeing how other households operate helps your child accept diversity and adapt to new situations.

Step 9: Give your children what they need, not what they want

When you are tired and harried and you know you might get angry if your children voice one more protest or ask you for one more thing, it's tempting to just give in to them. Perhaps they want to sleep in their clothes and refuse to change for bed. It's easy enough to give your assent; after all, it may mean you avoid losing your temper. Your anger, no matter what the cause, over-shadows everything else. Your children and your spouse focus on your behavior and forget any misbehavior that provoked it. It can be extremely difficult, when you are tired, to be firm and make your children observe a particular rule, whether it is getting dressed for bed, brushing teeth, or putting clothes in the laundry hamper. Think about what your own spiritual mentor or some-one you admire would do in this situation. Be patient. Tell your-self, "I am tired. I will find a little patience, somewhere." Take a deep breath and try to relax. Then send your children to do what they have to do, whatever it is.

Step 10: Take the good things from other religions (and leave the rest)

I know a person whose religious background will not be named to protect the innocent. She grew up with more don'ts than dos. She attended a religious school, lived in a neighborhood almost exclusively inhabited by families of her faith and, of course, attended religious services regularly. There was no television or secular literature in her home. At every turn, she was bombard-ed by rules: no drinking, no dancing, no smoking, no going to movies, and no playing cards.

Buddhism isn't like that. Even if most Buddhists agree on some underlying principles, how they are carried out in an individual's lifestyle is up to each individual. That can be good news for those who like freedom, but it can lead to uncertainty for those who yearn for guidance and direction. My best advice is to give your children all the information you can find. Help them to gather many options and understand them as completely as possible.

Once they make a decision, support them in experiencing the consequences. In retrospect, if it seems another choice would be wiser, show them by example that it's not shameful to admit a mistake and adjust your plans accordingly. Above all, remind your children that no two Buddhists (or Hindus, or Muslims, or Christians) are alike. We have all come to our own place in our own way. What works for the person sitting next to you at a teaching will not be right for you. Have the courage to ask good questions until you create a fit that's right for you.

To be truly alive is to be constantly open to new ideas. In fact, there is a glimmer of the spiritual in every experience. Be mindful of the world around you, both in the form of nature and in other people, so that you can be more connected to the spiritual inside yourself. The added bonus is that, as you help your child develop these characteristics, you'll deepen your own spiritual practices as well.

Resources

Childhood is a series of experiments in identity. Like trying on a variety of costumes at a masquerade, children assume attitudes that they change without warning. Most kids who describe themselves as Buddhists feel alone in their school or community. There are many ways to keep from being lonely and isolated. So-called "snail mail" still has its advantages. My daughters correspond with a student in an orphanage in India. In this day and age, being connected can be as easy as clicking a mouse. Check your search engine for key words such as "dharma" and "Buddha." Interesting chatrooms focused on Buddhist parenting also abound on the Internet. Finally, don't forget books that you can read alone or together with your child.

Recommended reading

The Dalai Lama. *My Land and My People: The Original Autobiography of His Holiness the Dalai Lama*. New York: Warner Books, 1987.

Eastoak, Sandy. *Dharma Family Treasures*. Berkeley: North Atlantic Books, 1994.

Fitzpatrick, Jean Grasso. *Something More: Nurturing Your Child's Spiritual Growth*. New York: Viking Press, 1991.

Hanh, Thich Nhat. *Old Path White Clouds: A Rich Source of Dharma Tales*. Berkeley: Parallax Press, 1991.

Hanh, Thich Nhat. *A Pebble for Your Pocket*. Berkeley: Parallax Press, 2001.

Hanh, Thich Nhat. *Under the Rose Apple Tree*. Berkeley: Parallax Press, 2002.

Jung, Betty. *The Kopan Cookbook: Vegetarian Recipes from a Tibetan Monastery.* San Francisco: Chronicle Books, 1992.

Kabat-Zinn, Myla and Jon Kabat-Zinn. *Everyday Blessings: The Inner Work of Mindful Parenting.* New York: Hyperion, 1998.

Metcalf, Franz. *Buddha in Your Backpack: Everyday Buddhism for Teens.* Berkeley: Ulysses Press, 2002.

Rimpoche, Gehlek. *Good Life, Good Death: Tibetan Wisdom on Reincarnation.* New York: Riverhead Books, 2002.

Rimpoche, Gehlek. *Odyssey to Freedom in 64 Steps.* Ann Arbor: Genden Editions, 1999.

Rosman, Steven M. *Spiritual Parenting: A Sourcebook for Parents and Teachers.* Wheaton: Quest Books, 1994.

Winston, Diana. *Wide Awake: A Buddhist Guide for Teens.* New York: Berkeley Publishing Group, 2003.

Bibliography

Berger, K. and T. Berger. *Ordinary Magic: Everyday Life as Spiritual Path.* Boston: Shambhala, 1992.

Eastoak, Sandy. *Dharma Family Treasures.* Berkeley: North Atlantic Books, 1994.

Gordon, Neil. "The Pity of Love." *Tricycle* (spring 2002): 69.

Jung, Betty. *The Kopan Cookbook: Vegetarian Recipes from a Tibetan Monastery.* San Francisco: Chronicle Books, 1992.

Kornfield, Jack, "Hindrances of the Householder (I)," Cherag's Library World Service *http://cheraglibrary.org/buddhist/kornfield/jkhindr1.htm.*

Landaw, J. and J. Brooke. *Prince Siddhartha: The Story of Buddha.* Boston: Wisdom, 1984.

Makransky, Lama John. "Cartoon as Path." *Tricycle* (fall 2001): 122.

Mercer, J. and H. Arlen. "Ac-cent-tchu-ate the Positive." New York: MPL Communications, Inc., 1940.

Rimpoche, Gehlek. *Good Life, Good Death: Tibetan Wisdom on Reincarnation*. New York: Riverhead Books, 2002.

Rimpoche, Gehlek. *Odyssey to Freedom in 64 Steps*. Ann Arbor: Genden Editions, 1999. (Available at the Jewel Heart store, 207 E. Washington Street, Ann Arbor, MI 48104, 734-994-3385.)

Rosman, Steven M. *Spiritual Parenting: A Sourcebook for Parents and Teachers*. Wheaton: Quest Books, 1994. Quoting Jack Kornfield, "A Parent's Guide to Conscious Childraising: Conscious Parenting," *Common Boundary* (January/February 1993): 24.

Thera, Soma. *The Way of Mindfulness: the Satipatthana Sutta and Its Commentary*. Kandy: Buddhist Publication Society, 1998.

Trungpa, Chogyam. *Cutting Through Spiritual Materialism*. Boston: Shambhala, 2002.

Woodward, F.L., trans. *Some Sayings of the Buddha*. London: Oxford University Press, 1973.

Other Ulysses Press mind/body titles

Buddha in Your Backpack: Everyday Buddhism for Teens
Franz Metcalf, $12.95
Especially written for teenagers, *Buddha in Your Backpack* explains Buddhism and shows how Buddha's teachings can add a little wisdom and sanity to their high-velocity lives.

Flip the Switch: 40 Anytime, Anywhere Meditations in 5 Minutes or Less
Eric Harrison, $10.95
Flip the Switch points out the time gaps that come throughout the day (idling at a red light, waiting for a computer to restart, standing in line at the grocery store) and teaches specially designed meditations that fit each of these situations.

What Would Buddha Do: 101 Answers to Life's Daily Dilemmas
Franz Metcalf, $9.95
This internationally popular book applies the wisdom of Buddha to everyday spiritual dilemmas including love, materialism, and self-image.

To order these books call 800-377-2542 or 510-601-8301, fax 510-601-8307, e-mail ulysses@ulyssespress.com, or write to Ulysses Press, P.O. Box 3440, Berkeley, CA 94703. All retail orders are shipped free of charge. California residents must include sales tax. Allow two to three weeks for delivery.

About the author

Greg Holden is a professional writer and editor. His best-known books include *Literary Chicago: A Book Lover's Tour of the Windy City*, *Internet Babylon: Secrets, Shocks, and Scandals on the Information Superhighway*, *Starting an Online Business for Dummies*, and *Creating Web Pages for Kids and Parents*. He lives with his two daughters, ages 10 and 12, in Chicago. A student of Tibetan Buddhism since 1989, he has edited a Buddhist newsletter and many books on Buddhism.